"Ora North brings a raw and powerful look at the reality of being an empath. It's not always glitter and unicorns; we must take a long, hard look at the wounds and shadows we hold; we must get real to heal. Ora skillfully guides us through this process so we can take off the spiritual mask and claim our true power as empaths."

—**Lisa Campion**, Reiki master teacher, and author of *The Art of Psychic Reiki*

"What a relief this book is! At turns fresh, familiar, frank, and funny, author Ora North manages to distill recovery models, cognitive behavioral therapy (CBT), and shamanism into a coherent and accessible program for empathy management, self-healing, and relationship building. Don't take the title seriously, though. After working the exercises in *I Don't Want to Be an Empath Anymore*, you will not only be more comfortable being so deep in the world of emotion, you will have become adept at it and found yourself embracing what an asset your sensitivities are to yourself and others. Highly recommended."

—**Kathryn L. Robyn**, healer, artist, author of *Spiritual Housecleaning*, and coauthor of *The Emotional House*

"Ora North is the wise, witchy aunt I never had, who has arrived on the scene just when this heartbroken world needs her most. How I wish I could've read this bracing tonic of a book when I was sixteen, and so overwhelmed by confusing, painful emotions that all I could do was bury them. Ora reassures us in her straight-talking way that it's never too late to witness and integrate our dark, scary feelings—and regain our equilibrium. Goddess bless her for doing this groundbreaking work, and for writing this compelling, enlightening book to empower sensitive souls like me!"

—**Simone Butler**, astrological consultant at www.astroalchemy.com, and author of *Moon Power* and *Astro Feng Shui*

"Ora North has penned an instant classic. *I Don't Want to Be an Empath Anymore* is the kind of book you immediately feel understood by; the kind of book that feels so perfect and obvious, you're a little surprised it didn't exist before it did. I devoured it and then gave it to my favorite people, because I wanted them to feel understood too."

—**Arden Leigh**, creator of The Re-Patterning Project, and frontwoman of Arden and the Wolves

"Ora tells the truth about what it means to be a deep-feeling person in this world. She blazes a way through the precarious world of self-inquiry, and she offers real-world tools that are restorative to the raw nerves of an empath. This book is a healing."

—**Erin Schroeder**, The Psychic Witch, psychic teacher

"As a 'cry of the millennial witch,' this guidebook has much to offer those who need to effectively harness the powers of empathetic sensitivities rather than be consumed by them. The author speaks volumes to the various aspects of being an empath in our culture, such as the dangers of the 'positive vibe only' complacency, past trauma, and the neglect of certain emotions. She offers innovative exercises such as listing your victims and villains of your shadow self, a formula to write your own pain alchemy affirmation, throwing yourself a pity party, and creating voluntary energetic blindness. Bravo, Ms. North!!"

—**Nancy Antenucci**, owner of Between Worlds LLC, author of the beloved *Psychic Tarot*, and teacher and presenter throughout the US and internationally as faculty for the Arcana Company in Chengdu, China

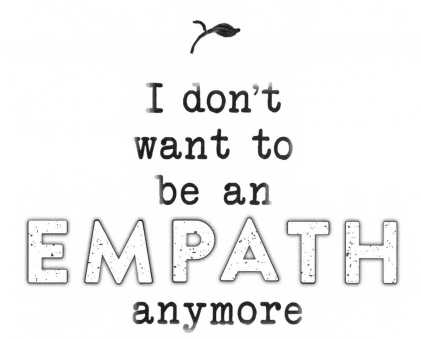

I don't want to be an EMPATH anymore

How to reclaim your
power over emotional overload,
maintain boundaries &
live your best life

ORA NORTH

REVEAL PRESS
AN IMPRINT OF NEW HARBINGER PUBLICATIONS

Publisher's Note

Distributed in Canada by Raincoast Books

Copyright © 2019 by Ora North
                 Reveal Press
                 An imprint of New Harbinger Publications, Inc.
                 5674 Shattuck Avenue
                 Oakland, CA 94609
                 www.newharbinger.com

Cover design by Sara Christian

Acquired by Jennye Garibaldi

Edited by Jean Blomquist

Text design by Michele Waters-Kermes and Tracy Carlson

Library of Congress Cataloging-in-Publication Data on file

Book printed in the United States of America

21   20   19

10   9   8   7   6   5   4   3   2   1   First Printing

For Katie, who felt too much.

Contents

Foreword

There is a rebel storyteller in all of us, I think, a submerged seer-poet who sits atop our ribs, skipping stones in our blood and waiting to be called up, hoping for the chance to climb our bones, stand on our tongue as if it were an orator's mound, and spill out wild truths that give pause to all who listen. The tales told by this deviant visionary are not those of skills mastered and quests fulfilled; they are those paradigm-shifting sorts of stories, riddled with shadow, uncertainty, and longing. That moment when we grant this outlaw the opportunity to speak is a wondrous initiation, one of those pivotal plot twists in our epic stories of becoming when we suddenly claim not only our socially valuable successes but also our as yet unmet desires to heal the many wounds of our foremothers.

A true elder-teacher, this storyteller is a sage healer who somehow—against all odds within this hard-edged society of ours where all things must be named and boxed—shares her experiences of unlearning and unease, stepping with grace into that rare role of a wise mentor who weaves hard-won knowledge with admitted, beauteous, and blessed uncertainty. Our aching world does not need another spiritual teacher who has solved every mystery, who floats far above the ground and is never in danger of falling. It is not the overbleached and all-knowing healer-prophet we seek; it is the wounded mystic who walks heavy on this ancient land, who has become the wild heart she needed when she was younger, and who tells stories not to offer soft-breasted comfort, not to rehash the old and outmoded, but, rather, to radically oppose the existing thought structures, change-resistant cultures, and socioeconomic systems that threaten to bind us all to joylessness.

True healing is never about a quick fix, and that mischievous maker of myths knows this well, as does Ora North. Healing happens only through awareness and integration, only by coming to terms with the gifts we have been given and the wounds that still pulse with the same ache our grandmothers' grandmothers nursed long ago on ancestral soil. What Ora offers in this book are not overly simplified tools or a diluted plan for winning at the Game of Empath. This book is an interactive wilderness guide of sorts, an eloquently written and sorely needed ownership manual for the empathic human soul.

As a Witch who believes our magick must be first and foremost a planet-savior during this desperate time of human history, I honor and bow to the work being done by empath-storytellers like Ora, who call out the "distortions of new age thinking" and frame empathy as not only a gift but one of the most valuable resources our ailing society can cultivate during the Anthropocene. She writes without making any one-size-fits-all claims about the potent medicine she offers, whilst being concurrently generous with tools, stories, and ample opportunities provided for the readers to draw their own conclusions about what it means to be an empath in a hard-hearted, trauma-riddled world.

When I first read Ora's writing years ago, I was struck by her ability to express with transparency the "cry of the millennial Witch," the exhaustion burdening the younger generation of magick-makers who are finding themselves hungry for an embodied kinship with the ancient and yet quite paradoxically without access to many compassionate elders who share their wisdom—*not* as immutable truths but as a lens, as an invitation. In this age when our prophets are few and our fears are many, it is often those healer-teachers who, regardless of linear age, harbor a hag's heart beneath their ribs, and Ora North is the crone-empath we all needed when we were babes. May you read her words as an invitation to come home to yourself, and may we all wake tomorrow more whole versions of the fractured souls we put to bed.

All blessings be.

—Danielle Dulsky
Author of *The Holy Wild: A Heathen Bible for the Untamed Woman* and *Woman Most Wild: Three Keys to Liberating the Witch Within*

Introduction

You must be exhausted. Aren't you?

You've always been sensitive. Maybe a little too sensitive.

You knew from a very early age that you felt a lot more than most people. You felt everything. Every life experience felt like an epic adventure, full of victorious highs and dangerous lows. How could they not see what you saw? How could they not understand the swinging pendulum of emotion that rose and fell within you each moment? There was a purity in the way you experienced the world, an amplified openness and curiosity that made you hyperaware of the joy and complexity and heartbreak of life. What gave others happiness, gave you pure ecstasy. What gave them disappointment, gave you heart-shattering pain. You have felt yourself moved from tears of pure joy to tears of desperate sadness all in the course of an afternoon. Sometimes you knew why you were feeling those things so intensely. Sometimes you didn't.

It didn't stop at you, though. No, this amplified way of being extended to others as well. Your sensitivity made it so you could feel and connect within your relationships just as intensely. Somehow a part of you just *knew* what other people were feeling, even when they didn't (or wouldn't) tell you. It was like wearing a second skin, made entirely of the thoughts and emotions of other people. This second skin was invisible, though; others never seemed to realize what you carried around day after day, year after year. So, you learned how to wear this second skin. You learned how to adapt to all the extra feelings.

Your ability to tune in to what your loved ones need, even without them telling you, has made you a beautifully nurturing human being. You can truly see the people you love, and you want more than anything to be there for them and to love them in the ways they need to be loved.

Seeing people like this also has its cost, though. The more you involve yourself with them, the more you willingly wear the second skin of everyone else's emotions, the more you get the energies—your own energy and the energy of others—confused. After a while, it's hard for you to tell which emotions belong to you and which emotions belong to them. The more those lines are blurred, the more you lose your confidence and the sense of your mission here on Earth. It could be that when your relationships go bad, they *really* go bad. The highs and lows that you experience with everything make your relationship problems feel like life or death. Resentments grow like weeds. You find yourself in this blurry place not only with your romantic relationships but also with your family. The emotional entanglements of ancestry weave through you, making it feel that it's impossible to untangle yourself and be free. Your suffering feels both slow and building, and immediate and explosive. You see only your loved ones' emotions. Where did yours go, anyway? You're not really sure. But being able to see everyone else for their emotions leaves you feeling oddly lonely in your own feelings.

Everyone comes to you for advice and help, but where is *your* advice? Where is *your* help?

Even though your sensitivity lends to your emotional intelligence, working can be a challenge. The emotional labor you put in at your job, for issues that are not yours, drains your energy and your spirit. Maybe it feels like there's nothing you can do to be noticed for your work and get ahead, and you begin making yourself smaller to accommodate your coworkers and supervisors. You might even make excuses for their bad behaviors because you can feel the pain they operate from. Perhaps you think, *Well, I'll just let this one time slide,* until you realize that years have passed and that one time has multiplied into countless times. You've watched everyone else move forward, propelled by your compassion and empathy for them, and yet you're still standing still.

When you come home at night, after your draining work experience, maybe you find yourself immediately immersed in the care of your significant other or your kids. You sigh without complaining most of the time, slipping into the caretaker role that they never seem to see or appreciate. You might have an emotionally detached conversation with your partner, because at this point, you don't even know how to express the overwhelming nature of your feelings. Feeling unseen, you might turn on the TV to decompress. All you want to do is relax, but every show you see is filled with violence or cruelty, and you find yourself shaking. You simply can't handle more sadness, more pain. You may find yourself going to bed utterly exhausted—and no wonder you're exhausted.

This is the life of the overwhelmed empath. It's one of frustration, of loneliness, of sensitivity gone sideways. Eventually, this life ruins your relationships and your career, and leaves you completely drained of vitality. It makes you wish you weren't an empath anymore.

Living this way isn't sustainable, but sometimes it's the only lifestyle you can imagine. Sometimes you don't realize there's another option.

3

From Exhausted to Empowered

I do see another option for the overwhelmed empath. I see you as a strong, empowered human being using your sensitivity as your superpower.

Instead of relationships that get messy and confusing and painful, I see you standing strong in your boundaries, able to clearly define what energy is yours and what energy is theirs. Instead of being ignored or taken advantage of, I see you excelling at your work, speaking your truth, and being unashamed for it. I see you taking time to rest, filling up your energy reserves with intention. I see you processing through your painful emotions, becoming a container for amazing healing and change in this world. I see you getting what you truly deserve, simply because you're strong enough to say it, to take it, to be it.

Your relationships are easier, because you know exactly what you need and how to get it. Your energy comes back in full force, because you know how to protect it. You don't even worry about the energy vampires of the world, because you know yourself too well to let even the thought of them bother you. You have found another path for yourself: a path of ease, grace, and clarity.

I know it might sound impossible, and I know change is scary, even when you desperately crave it. Self-growth isn't easy, and when it involves the darker emotions of being an empath, it's even harder. But as I enter these words into these pages, I put this promise within them: if you stay with me throughout these chapters and face the things that come up, you *will* find a strength in yourself you've never known.

You will say hello to the fears that hide inside of you. You will say hello to your childhood pain and your conditioning. And because of your willingness to see your fears and your pain, you will also say hello to your primal power, your inner wise self, and your flawless intuition.

You are an amazing person with the potential to change lives—both your own life and the lives of others. This sensitivity you have, which seems to betray you on a daily basis, can be understood on a deeper level and can unlock your higher self in a way you've only dreamed about.

This book is an emotional journey. It will guide you down the path of emotional shadow work, encouraging you to dig into all of your messy energy and all of your pain. The only way out of the pain is *through* it, and the practices in this book will guide you to the other side.

You'll make your relationships a hell of a lot easier by being able to differentiate between the energy of others and your own, and by being able to nurture and strengthen the boundaries that protect those relationships. You'll receive the respect you deserve from the people in your life by being able to show up in all your glory, taking up the space you rightfully deserve. Everything in your life will seem simpler and more straightforward because of the complicated work you are showing up for right now.

Thank you for showing up. Showing up is half the battle.

A Journey into Your Truest Self

What you'll do in this book requires courage, because the scariest thing you could face in this lifetime is the truth about yourself and your power. You'll open up a door you've been trying to keep shut, and you'll step through it. You'll dive into your emotions and learn a new way to handle them. You'll meet your emotions with love and acceptance, even if they're negative emotions. You'll identify your patterns and the roots of your pain, and you'll transmute them into personal power.

5

First, we'll look at what the hell an empath is, and some of the ways being an empath has made life a little more difficult. We'll shift the focus of being an empath from your relationships with other people to your relationship with *yourself*.

Then, we'll explore the shadow side of being an empath. Being able to approach and work with your own personal darkness as much as you work with the light will completely change how you see yourself and the world. We'll learn how to appreciate the parts of you that live in that hidden shadow self and the parts of you that were wounded in childhood. These parts are full of power, and yet we've been taught to ignore them all our lives.

Once we've worked with your shadow self and your childhood wounds, we'll talk about all the emotions you experience all the time. Emotions are simply energetic messages, and you're going to learn how to energetically identify and track your emotions, as well as translate the messages they bring. You'll use your intuition to work with those energies in a new and healing way. And because you'll be able to identify the energies of your own emotions, you will always be able to differentiate between your own emotions and the emotions of others.

You'll also use these tools when we look into boundaries and relationships. I'll show you a game-changing trick for creating amazing boundaries, and you'll learn how to work with your boundaries in a way that protects you from the bad stuff but also leaves you open for the good stuff. These tools will help when you look into the different dynamics an empath faces in relationships. Identifying emotional and energetic patterns in relationships will make your life easier, because you'll know what to do to honor yourself.

Often in this process of emotional shadow work, some latent trauma and past sorrows will come up as you explore

6

yourself and your shadow side. This is normal. I'll show you how to deal with the trauma that comes up, and I'll also encourage you to seek support for that trauma when it feels like it's too much. One of our goals is to turn your sorrows into treasures, and to do that, we'll approach your sorrows in a helpful, new way. There are always obstacles in our path when we're trying to accomplish something big and life-changing, and this process is no different. I'll show you some obstacles you may face, and I swear they're the same obstacles I've faced myself, the same obstacles that so many empaths have faced. No one is immune to obstacles, but we can choose how to handle them.

I will give you tools to assist you in cleansing your energy, tools you can use for the rest of your life. If you're new to working with energy, Energetics 101 in the resource section will introduce you to how energetics work. You'll also find Energetic Clearing Tools in the resource section. You'll be able to employ a variety of techniques to create space for yourself, cleanse yourself of everyone else's energy, and get to know the most important person in this process: you!

When you and others do this work, each person will come away with something a little bit different. I offer many different tools and approaches in the coming chapters, and each one will hit you in a unique way. There is no right or wrong way to feel, and I want to give you multiple ways to approach, befriend, and heal the hidden parts of yourself. I know how difficult it is to be an empath, especially an overwhelmed empath. I know what's at stake, and how each experience with each empath tells a beautifully complex story, so I'm here to give you a tool belt so you can use whatever tools work best with your own process. What you need to make this work successful is your curiosity—your willingness to see yourself in your shadows and how they might help you.

As I've written this book, I've imagined you. I've imagined where you might be as you're reading this—what's going on in your life, what your goals are. I've cried as I've imagined the pain you've lived through as an overwhelmed empath. I've rejoiced as I've imagined the beauty of your life purpose. All of this has been for you. More than anything, I want you to be able to live your life as an empowered empath, doing what you came to this planet to do.

DO THE WORK

Throughout the book, you will find exercises and writing prompts. Recording your thoughts and responses is a great way to open the door to your own healing and self-discovery. This book relies heavily on the practice of journaling, so I encourage you to get a journal for these practices (more on that below). I also understand that some people aren't really the journaling type, and that's okay too. If that's you, I encourage you to use your phone or other recording device to speak your thoughts openly for each exercise and writing prompt. You can then refer back to your own words as you process deeper. As long as you're taking the time and space for each activity, it will have a huge impact.

8

Choose a Journal

If you decide to use a journal, find one that's your favorite color, or one that has a cover design that you love. If you love the way your journal looks, you'll be more likely to use it. Also get the kind of pens or pencils that you like. If you're like me, using a specific brand of pen makes writing more enjoyable for you. No matter what kind of journal and pen you like, setting aside time for reading and journaling your experiences is going to make this work even more powerful.

CHAPTER 1

What the Hell Is an Empath?

The root feeling of empathy is most often pain. Emotional pain is usually the first indication for an empath that something strange is happening. For whatever reason, for many empaths, pain and negative emotions are sensed more strongly and more easily than joy and positive emotions. It's not that we don't sense joy and positive emotions, but joy doesn't energetically grasp at us in the same way. Joy doesn't desperately grapple for compassion the way that suffering does. Joy radiates and spreads gently and warmly, like a swift sunrise over a soft meadow. Pain, on the other hand, stabs the lungs like falling into cold water. When another being is suffering, it's like their energy is calling out to the void from the freezing waters, reaching for a hand that could pull them to safety. Empaths feel that call more than anything else.

I was once at an event with a friend of mine, another spiritual-type person. She had just introduced me to another woman in the community. As I spoke with this woman, I was shocked by how heartbroken I felt. I had the visual of her heart being filled with broken shards of glass, and the shards seemed to pierce my own heart, even as we engaged in pleasant conversation.

As she walked away, I clutched my chest and said to my friend, "Wow. Her heart is so heavy and sad."

My friend told me that the woman was going through a divorce, but added scornfully, "You're so negative all the time."

Her icy and disapproving tone shocked me, though this wasn't the first time I'd felt judged for my empathic leanings. I couldn't help that I was feeling the heartbreak of that woman. I couldn't help that my own heart ached from a story I wasn't even a part of.

My friend's reaction to my empathy hurt. As she described her dislike of my negativity, I felt myself build an emotional wall between us, and our friendship was never the same. I felt an overwhelming amount of isolation, all because I had been emotionally connected to a stranger.

Herein lies the paradox of empathy: being connected to the emotions of others leaves an empath incredibly isolated. There is a deep well of loneliness that comes with the ability to tap into the pulse of everyone's emotions. Your own emotions are often left buried and unseen, especially since, for someone to truly see you and see your pain, they would also have to see you *seeing the pain of everyone else*. That's a tall order for any human being.

The pain of being unseen as an empath is overwhelming and disruptive. These kinds of experiences leave us feeling like being an empath is something we've been cursed with. But it doesn't have to be that way. You can take that pain and learn how to turn your curse into a blessing. But to do that, we first need to understand what exactly an empath is and how your empath nature manifests in your life. Once you can see the common patterns that emerge as a result of the wounds of being highly sensitive, once you embrace the pain of your experience, you can then take that awareness and turn it toward self-empowerment. By understanding the curse of being an empath, you can work with your pain and turn it into a blessing.

11

Empath Nature 101

"Empath" is a term that has been gaining popularity. In a world where our feelings are more important than ever, and our society bites back at the need for vulnerability, sensitive souls have rallied around the experience of being an empath. In its most simplistic terms, an *empath* is someone who feels the emotions of others, someone whose identity is emotionally interwoven with others. While empathy itself can be a learned skill on a spectrum, an empath is born with those skills. You are either an empath or you're not, and if you're reading this book, I'm going to assume that you definitely are. Here are some of the common signs of being an empath:

- You experience sensitivity toward other people.

- You have the ability to feel the emotions of others without being told.

- You experience strange pains in the body that may mimic the pain of another.

- You feel extreme sensitivity to violence, gore, and cruelty.

- You are a healer or an aspiring healer.

- You know things about people before being told.

- You have strong emotional reactions (good or bad) to music, movies, books, and other things.

- You have a natural ability for working with children and animals. They are drawn to you.

- People tend to share their secrets with you for no reason, even if they don't know you.

- You're drawn to nature.

- You can physically feel energy.

- You experience bouts of rage or tears that may or may not be your own.

- You have accurate dreams about the past or future of a person.

- You are sensitive to food and your environment. You may have food allergies or chemical sensitivities.

- You are easily overwhelmed in crowds.

Though the empath has often been credited as a divine being with supernatural powers, it's actually quite common. The gap between the divine and the mundane is not as wide as one would think. It's more like a messy overlap of varying degrees than a gap, really. More of us have stuck our hands in the cosmic cookie jar than we even realize.

What could possibly be normal about feeling the emotions of others? Well, human beings are creatures who live and make choices based on their emotions. What feels good and what doesn't feel good are basic driving forces of the human life. Change is created through emotion in action. (How many times have you made a decision based on what your emotions were telling you?) Empaths are simply people with the natural ability to feel much more emotion and energy than others, even extending past their own lives and experiences. They cannot only feel how their own life has changed based on their emotions, but they can feel how others make choices based on emotions as well. I might even argue that a conscious empath could create more change in the world than anyone else, because they would have a working understanding of how people operate and what motivates them.

Stuck in the Service Role

If you look at the list of signs above, you may notice that most of them are related to other people. This makes sense, as we often define our empath nature by how we experience the

13

emotions of others and how we internalize what is outside of ourselves. Our ability to deeply feel the experiences and feelings of other people is technically what makes us empaths. This naturally puts us in the position to be wonderful healers, teachers, counselors, mothers, and caretakers, because we understand how other people are feeling better than anyone else.

However, because of our natural tendency toward caring for others, the label "empath" has been idealized as a steward of the world, an expression of divine service, a holy badge of honor. It is known to be the ultimate sacred sacrifice, to live for others. To feel what they're feeling so you can give them what they need. To put their needs above your own. This is partially true. We all know this. Being of service to others is truly a beautiful gift to the world.

But while it's true that being of service is a necessary role for the world, it also comes with its own dangers for the empath. The trouble with the view of the empath as the servant is that the reference points of our entire identities are placed within the emotions of others as a result. This would mean that your purpose only exists inside of other people and their expectations and feelings. Anytime you find that your identity is built on the feelings of others, you will probably find yourself on some shaky ground. The more we identify ourselves as empaths through our experiences with others rather than our experience with ourselves, the more we give away our personal power, both consciously and unconsciously.

We literally define ourselves through others when we speak of empaths. We pigeonhole ourselves into a service role where we lack autonomy, self-empowerment, and freedom of choice. Can you think of situations in your own life where your purpose has been decided by how someone else feels about your role in their life?

14

When we define ourselves through others, even with Mother-Teresa-like intentions, we are at the mercy of the tides of emotions that aren't even our own. If you are an empathic mother, you might find yourself deciding your value based on the actions and attitudes of your children, which is guaranteed to disappoint you at times. If you are an empathic healer, you might find yourself swinging wildly between the highs and lows of your clients' healing, losing your own center in the process. If you are in a committed relationship, the quality of your life may be decided by however your partner feels about you in that moment.

To be fair, we all rely on others to decide the quality of our lives in some way. We all are deeply affected by the emotions of others, and that's normal and healthy. All the best relationships are a constant conversation about shifting emotions. However, when we hold the emotions of others responsible for our own happiness, or decide the usefulness of ourselves based on what we can give others emotionally, we screw ourselves over in the process. Not only do we end up unconsciously holding other people hostage emotionally, but we become miserable martyrs in the process. You may find yourself keeping a mental tally of all the times you've set yourself aside to meet the emotional needs of others, waiting for the moment they will even the score by being of service to you in the same way. When the people we rely on are not delivering our happiness, when they're not evening the score, that's when the resentment starts to build.

But look at everything I'm doing for them! Look at everything I'm sacrificing for them! They should do the same. Why aren't they doing the same?! How did I end up here?!

If that sounds like you in some of your relationships, don't feel bad. I've said those things countless times about countless people. (And I'm a Leo, so I've been *really* dramatic about it.)

15

The weird thing about empathy is that it can turn on you. The more you remain in service to others, while secretly hoping for them to return the favor by being in service to you as well, the more you let the beauty of your empathy rot away in your chest. Sacrificing your own personal journey for the sake of others, waiting for someone to do the same for you, isn't the holy badge of honor that it's made out to be.

There is nothing sacred about losing yourself disguised as a holy mission.

In my first two years of working as a shamanic healer, it was strange to feel how easy it was to tap into the pain and the beauty of my clients during soul retrieval sessions. I loved journeying for them and finding their lost inner children. I loved bringing them back for integration and experiencing the wholeness of their being. It came naturally, and I was blessed and grateful for the chance to connect with others in such an intimate way, despite the pain I often felt during a session.

At the same time, however, I was really buying into my label as a "healer" and what that was supposed to mean about me. Healers were supposed to be Zen. Healers were not supposed to be damaged or angry. They weren't supposed to be feeling pain as often as I was. They weren't supposed to be so intense and moody like I was. Healers were supposed to be living examples of drama-free perfection.

Because of what I thought I was supposed to be, I pushed away years of pain, thinking it was the right thing to do for my clients and for the world, the *spiritual* thing to do. I focused only the positive and pushed away my own darkness. Eventually, I found myself jealous of my own clients. I relied on them for my own healing and was disappointed when it didn't happen that way. *Why do they get healing and I don't? Why can't I be seen like that? Why can't I be healed too?* Even

16

though I was genuinely helping others, I became so bitter and so unsatisfied that I finally couldn't take it anymore. I'd become a slave and a martyr to the "healer" role, thinking that living for others would be enough for me.

I had what I call my "screw it" moment. I got real honest about myself and what I needed. I acknowledged that I had years of hurt inside my bones. My cells remembered. I could not and would not wrap up my hurt, put a pretty Zen-master bow on it, and give it away to the world as "a gift."

I was not and am not a sacrificial lamb.

Neither are you.

Have you reached your "screw it" moment? Have you been pushing your pain away for years, just waiting for someone to give you the same kind of love that you give everyone else? Have you been craving the same kind of healing and presence that you so often provide for others? More than that, are you ready to do the "selfish" thing and let go of your servant's role so you can discover what it truly means to be alive in this world as an empath?

17

For me, that meant that I stopped working with clients for two full years, vowing only to work with myself until my own needs were met and my cup was full again. I quit my servant's role so I could figure out how to be an empath without losing myself in others or without deciding my own worth based on what I could do for them. What will this mean for you? What does it look like to step away from that role, even a little bit? At the end of this chapter, you'll have the opportunity to journal about your roles and how it feels to pull away from them.

The truth is that you cannot truly be of lasting service to others until you are in service to yourself. The true gift of being an empath is not in your connection to others, but in your connection to yourself as a powerful and liberated force of nature. You have the power to fill your own cup and meet your own needs.

Your gifts do not make you a sacrificial lamb. Your sensitivity does not make you a martyr. You are more than that. If you deny yourself your autonomy, you deny the world of what it truly needs: *you*.

Validating Your Feelings

The isolation you feel as an empath can make it very difficult to feel like your pain is being seen by others. Since it's impossible for others to see the full extent of that pain, even when they want to, it's incredibly important for you to be willing to see your *own* pain.

More than anything else, feelings simply want to be witnessed and validated. Feelings are fluid and passing, but that doesn't mean they aren't important or powerful. (Our world is run by emotions, remember?) I often use the metaphor that feelings are like a toddler experiencing the world, calling out for Mom to watch.

Mom, look! I'm doing a spin.

Mom, look! I fell down on the stairs.

Mom, look! My finger is hurt.

Mom, look! I drew a picture.

If Mom looks, the toddler feels seen and validated that they are learning and experiencing life. Mom doesn't necessarily need to do anything in response. Sometimes Mom will need to bandage up a wound or embrace her child in her arms, but other times nodding and saying, "I see that, wow!" is enough for her to make her child feel validated and happy. However, if Mom completely ignores the child, the child feels isolated and alone in their experience of the world.

Our feelings work the same way. They show us that our spirits are still as pure as a toddler's, diving into the raw experiences of life and reacting to them. As we grow into adults, we lose the value of emotions in favor of logic and expectation, and we stop witnessing the feelings of others and of ourselves. This is especially true with pain. In a culture that promotes binary emotional landscapes, we are expected to highly praise and validate success and happiness, while hiding, disguising, or invalidating pain. We've been trained to push that pain away. We've been trained to be the mother who refuses to look when her child calls.

Not witnessing your pain can permanently alter the landscape of your life, like a toddler who is ignored for too long. In the Do the Work section of this chapter, you'll be invited to start seeing and validating all of your emotions.

19

The Art and Practice of Your Empathic Gift

Ah, there is this beautiful moment, this magnificent point in time when you have released everything you have into the wind, and you not only feel everything, but you also feel nothing. You feel perfectly held and perfectly free. You have found that axis point where creation and destruction meet, and no effort whatsoever is needed. You are reaching and receiving, and simultaneously letting go and offering. You are calm and complete, and yet so amused and touched by your own intricacies.

This is the spirit of art.

This is the gift of authentic expression.

This is the gift of creative flow.

This is a gift that's available to you as an empath.

In the same way that a painter paints and a writer writes, an empath feels. The act of feeling, for an empath, is not just a by-product of other people, but a solitary art. The empath is not just a sponge for other people. The empath is a solitary artist.

When you pull yourself away from everyone else, when you find yourself alone with your own mind and your own heart, when you pour out all the feelings you have been brimming over with, you find something incredible. You find the true core feeling of being an empath: the deep, mysterious, wild emptiness of nature and creation. Here, everything and anything is possible. Here, you move mountains with your mind and sink ships with a song. You build cities from ash and make flowers bloom with your sex. You open minds and change hearts and serve justice on a platter. Anything and everything is within your power.

This might seem like a far cry from the overwhelmed and unseen empath you may be accustomed to being, but I assure you, it's inside of you. You see, a funny thing happens when you begin to witness your own pain. The more you honestly witness and validate the pain you feel, the more your pain wants to go to work for you. When your pain feels truly seen, it wants to transmute itself into something beautiful and productive. In the same way that you would treat your feelings as a toddler—simply desiring to be witnessed—you can treat your feelings as an artist, looking for an avenue to express yourself creatively.

As you read this book, keep this in mind: inside of you is a deep well of creation, and you are a solitary artist of feeling. We'll talk a lot about your experiences with other people and their feelings, and how your empathy has royally messed up

20

your life, as those are things that are here to be witnessed and validated. In many ways, being an empath really is like being a sponge for other people's feelings and experiences. But you are so much more than that, and my real hope is for you to go beyond and through your experience of others, into that point of transmutation and creation. My real hope is for you to start seeing yourself as that solitary artist, forever curious about the way *you* experience the world and the way *you* feel about this weird experience as a human. In doing this, you will discover your art of feeling, and through your art, you will find your truth and your mission. In your art of feeling, you will find yourself as you were always meant to be.

DO THE WORK

What if you could strip away all the labels and roles you have taken on as an empath? What if you peeled away the mother, the healer, the teacher, the husband, the daughter, the artist, the brother? What would you be? What would be left of your purpose? Would the very existence of "empath" disappear without those roles to play for others? Who would you be? And what would happen if you named and validated all your feelings? These exercises will help you answer those questions.

Name Your Labels

In your journal, make a list of all the labels in your life, whether they are self-appointed labels or given to you by others. Include all of them: the positive, the negative, and the neutral.

Take a look at your list, and notice how many of them are given to you because of your relationship to other people. Notice how many of them are used to explain your social position in life.

One by one, cross out each label, as if they don't exist anymore. With each one you cross out, imagine that label doesn't apply to you and notice how you feel. Imagine that the purpose you have within each label dissolves from the world as you cross it out. Does it feel good to let that purpose dissolve? Is it a relief? Does it feel terrible to lose it? Notice each feeling you have.

When you have every label crossed out, sit in the idea that none of those things make you who you are. If you're not those things, *who are you*? Journal your answer to that question, allowing yourself to express your reactions, no matter how positive or negative they may be.

Name Your Feelings

At the end of the day, take your journal out and write about all the feelings you felt during your day. Try to remember from first waking up until this point. Write down every feeling you can remember, no matter how insignificant it may seem.

At the start of the next day, commit to carrying your journal with you. Every time you consciously experience a feeling, jot it down in your journal. You can decide if you'll explain the reason for your feelings in your journal or not, but make sure to write down each one as you experience it, even if you experience a feeling more than once.

Now compare the two days. If you did the exercise with as much effort as you could, you'll find that your second list is much longer than your first. You'll realize that it's nearly impossible to write down each and every feeling as it happens throughout the day because there are so many. On the second day, you were asked to be much more present with your feelings as you were feeling them; whereas on the first day, you probably only remembered the prominent ones, letting most of the feelings slip through unnoticed.

The point is that unless we are intentionally trying to be present with our emotions, we let most of them slip by unseen, or worse, we tell ourselves not to feel them. This exercise can illuminate how unexplored our emotional landscapes can be, and how our upbringing and our culture can condition us to believe they're of no importance or value.

22

Every feeling you wrote down, however small or insignificant, came from either a place of internal strength or internal wounding, or a combination of the two. Those sources of feeling are what rule you day in and day out, whether you realize it or not. They make decisions for you, they embark on relationships for you, they find and lose opportunities for you. They operate on conditioned neural pathways, not conscious choice. Pay special attention to the "bad" feelings on your list, and refrain from judging yourself on how many of them there are. This is an opportunity to check in with the hidden pain you feel on a daily basis.

Wouldn't you like to be more involved in your life? Wouldn't you like to understand yourself so well that you could confidently be the master of your own fate? You may not be able to journal every feeling you have every moment, but you can certainly increase your awareness of those feelings and be able to notice and acknowledge them as you move throughout your day. You can begin to shift how many of your feelings you allow yourself to experience, and honor the ones you would usually push away.

CHAPTER 2

No Light Without Darkness

"**S**o you're an empath too?" she asked, smiling sweetly.

"I nodded, returning a meek smile of my own as I stroked the edges of my coffee cup cautiously. I couldn't remember why I'd agreed to this meeting. Curiosity, perhaps. Her social media platform was one covered with glitter, unicorns, and positive thinking. She wore a white T-shirt that read *MAKE MAGIC HAPPEN*. She signed her e-mails with *xoxo Love and Light*.

"That's so awesome," she replied, tossing her perfectly curled blonde hair. "Isn't it such a gift? It's so much easier to work with people and help them see their own light. I mean, I'm also a psychic medium, so I have an extra edge, but being an empath is so great."

I cringed imperceptibly at her words. For the briefest moment, I wanted to hold her face in my hands and shake the glitter out of her brain.

I couldn't tolerate another "spiritual" person telling me about the gift of being an empath. If this was such a gift, why was I so jaded? *Did a gift receipt come with this? What's the return policy? Did I lose my place in line at the shiny, trendy, law-of-attraction-mala-bead-wearing-Bali-traveling-Reiki-master shop?*

How could I tell this bubbly spirit-entrepreneur that being an empath was an unspeakable and unbearable burden? How could I explain that every time I connected to the inner pain of my friends and loved ones and strangers, I instantly burst into tears over the raw intensity of that pain? How could I tell her that her words lacked authenticity in her positivity, that I wanted *more* from her? More honesty. More realness.

"Yeah, it can be," I finally answered in an even tone, processing my inner dialogue on my own.

I waited for her to tap into my true feelings, to feel the reality of the other end of this conversation, to use her empath skills to discern the truth of the pain I felt. But she didn't. She carried on, talking about one of her clients that she had recently helped and how the universe conspired to bring them together. She gushed about the law of attraction and manifesting abundance and how important it was to be a warrior for the Light.

She stopped, looking up past my shoulder for a moment. "Your guides are telling me there's something you need, and that you and I were meant to meet for this reason," she stated seriously. "Maybe to do some life coaching with me. Let me tell you about this package I'm offering..."

My guides most certainly don't talk to strangers, I thought. But I kept that to myself.

After all, I was no "psychic medium." I was just an empath.

There's a tendency to only focus on the positive and the light with self-growth, to only embrace the side that manifests abundance and makes magic happen, but the most important aspect of working with your empath nature is being able to work with your personal shadow. Without acknowledging your darkness, your self-growth is stunted by half. When you learn to balance both the light and dark in equal measure, and you know how to navigate the new age distortions, your path forward toward self-realization is more grounded, more powerful, and, ultimately, more real.

Real People Have Shadows

Most of the new age platitudes that have gained popularity in the last decade have shared the same basic message: stay in the Light at all costs, don't let yourself stray into the darkness, and focus on positivity all the time to raise your vibration.

How can we stay in the Light all the time when half of our lives are literally spent in the dark? At the end of each day, night inevitably falls, and when it does, it brings a whole new landscape into view. Beautiful creatures of the night emerge, and the world is dimly lit with stars and moonlight. Things that looked one way in the stark light of day transform into a completely different scene. The darkness allows us to see things in a different way, and the same goes for our own darkness.

It was the famous Swiss psychiatrist and psychoanalyst Carl Jung, who developed the concept of the *shadow archetype*, which he described as "the unconscious aspect of the personality which the conscious ego does not identify in itself." Basically, your shadow is made up of the parts of you that aren't as desirable as the "good" parts. It's your dark side, and it's likely that you've been taught that your dark side must be rejected or ignored completely.

We all have a dark side, and pretending we don't doesn't actually make it go away. In fact, the more you reject your own darkness, the more it will find a sneaky way to infiltrate your actions. If you don't befriend it and allow it space, it will manipulate you for its own purpose.

If you find yourself following self-destructive patterns for no reason, that's your shadow creeping out. If you lash out at your loved ones in an uncharacteristic way, that's your shadow creeping out. If you find yourself unconsciously self-sabotaging every good move you try to make, that's your shadow creeping out. If you find yourself always looking for the upper hand in your relationships, that's your shadow creeping out. If you feel irritated and claustrophobic regularly, that's a sign your shadow is expanding to a point your body can no longer contain it.

When you choose to consciously work with your shadow instead, you will be able to break your self-destructive patterns and discontent. Knowing and dealing with your own darkness will also give you the insight and discernment to deal with other people's darkness, which is an essential skill for the empath. If you do not have the eyes to see yourself, you will certainly be blind to others.

Carl Jung also described the shadow self as "the seat of creativity." He believed the shadow encompassed not only the unconscious negative parts, but also the unconscious positive parts. Some of our greatest gifts and greatest strengths can only be uncovered when we willingly uncover our weaknesses and pain first.

Connecting with your shadow self could be one of the biggest turning points in your journey as an empath.

Lightwashing: Choose Your Own Adventure

In a world now overrun with gurus touting the divinity in positive thinking and the law of attraction and manifesting abundance, the real gritty bits inside of ourselves are being completely overlooked or, worse, intentionally dismissed. I began to use the term "lightwashing" to describe the act of taking any real emotion that may be difficult and covering it with trite displays of affirmations, positivity memes, rainbows and unicorns, and fake smiles. This is the bubbly twenty-something life coach who tells you that your boyfriend abuses you because your vibration is too low, or the handsome meditation expert who tells you that your desire for love is simply a manifestation of your insecurity, or—*my favorite*—the healers who tell you that you must kill your ego to become truly enlightened. In the quest to become enlightened beings, we've idealized the nonhuman and demonized the human, effectively promoting the idea that we must rid ourselves of our humanness to be spiritual masters.

Emotions, unfortunately, fall into the category of human-ness. This means that emotions, mostly the "negative" ones, are included in the things we should get rid of on our way to enlightenment. This is especially bad news for empaths, since they feel all the emotions all the time. How tragic to hear that the primary way you experience your life is something you need to get rid of!

One of the ways you can empower yourself as an empath is by connecting more with your humanness, and seeing it as part of the whole of divinity rather than separate from it. Lightwashing will not work for you. Positive thinking to cover up your bad feelings will not work for you. You need to *feel*. You need to feel it all.

The Distortions of New Age Thinking

30   There are a few common new age distortions perpetuated by gurus and teachers today, and they are all guilty of lightwash-ing. Let's break them down.

Always focus on the present and the Now.

While being as present as possible is usually a good thing, you can't truly focus on the Now if your painful past is still calling. Having unresolved issues from your past will prevent you from being able to stay present, and will actually skew your view of your life.

When you first face your past and the scary emotions you find there, you then can clear out that persistent energy and focus on the present in a healthy and rewarding way. If those things aren't cleared, they will crowd you so much that you won't even have room for the Now. This is especially impor-tant for empaths, since every experience brings with it its own deeply felt emotion, and if you don't deal with those emotions, they'll continue to color the experience of your Now.

If you're feeling sad, use positive affirmations.

Sometimes affirmations work. Sometimes they can help shift your thoughts into more productive ones. With deeper wounds, however, those affirmations could potentially make your negative thoughts and feelings worse.

If you have a very strong negative thought, one that's been perpetuating its own negative cycle for years, you may find that using a positive affirmation that is *so* far from the truth will create an energetic dissonance that you can't bridge. That dissonance sets you up to fail, and creates even more distance between where you really are now and where you want to go. It's much harder to reach your destination if you're lying to yourself about your starting point. That feeling of dissonance, of lying to yourself, is especially strong for empaths. Since empaths need validation for their feelings more than anything else, they need a different kind of affirmation. In the Do the Work section of this chapter, you'll have the chance to use affirmations that will work better for your sensitive nature.

31

We are all one.

This one is especially tricky, since it's very real on one level. The fact that we are all magically connected in one big web of existence is true. But we are also here as humans, and humans are as individual as they can come. We all have incredibly unique personalities, genes, upbringings, life experiences, and interests.

The "we are one" distortion is often used to dismiss the painful experience of the individual in favor of the larger, more enlightened experience. When this is done on such a large scale, it takes away the importance of individual story-telling and growth, which takes away the juiciness of personal evolution. This particular concept is also usually pretty guilty of sexism and racism.

It's detrimental for an empath to have their individual experience taken away and lost within the idea of oneness. The empath needs to feel separate from the messiness of others before they can use oneness as a helpful spiritual ideal. On the flip side, it can also be detrimental for an empath to subscribe to oneness with others. Because empaths can feel the pain of others so easily, there's the possibility that the empath could overlook the individual experience and story of the other person, bypassing *their* need for validation. While many people on earth have the primary spiritual mission of merging with others into oneness, empaths have already come with the inherent ability and compulsion to do that. In their case, their mission is first to be able to separate from everyone else and see themselves in their independence before striving for oneness. Empaths are always the first to experience the shadow side of oneness.

Emotions aren't important, so ignore them and let them pass.

There are many who say you should be as neutral as possible about your emotions, to the point where it's healthier to ignore them and focus on something else instead. They'll say that emotions aren't real. Or that you are not your emotions, so you shouldn't give them attention. While awareness and neutrality are important energetic tools, and ones we'll get into later, ignoring your feelings is certainly not the same as being neutral.

32

While you should let your emotions pass, since emotions are fluid and constantly changing, you should feel them first. Feel them like waves washing over you. Just because the wave will soon go away, doesn't mean that the wave isn't real and that it's not having an effect on you.

Your reaction to other people is all about you and not them.

This is the "we are all just mirrors" distortion. It's true that we often see things in other people that reflect where we're at in our own journeys, but this isn't always the case. There are those who will say that someone is being mean to you because they're picking up on how you yourself are mean, so it's really all about you and the other party can't be held responsible.

This is a convenient way to blame the victim, and it can also be used in predatory ways for manipulative ends. Sometimes what you see in others is really just a reflection of yourself. Really though, sometimes someone being a jerk to you is really just because they're a jerk. That doesn't mean that you can't find pieces of your reflection in everyone you meet, but to assume everyone is just a reflection of yourself (whether that reflection is flattering or not) breeds narcissism.

For an empath, there's already enough difficulty figuring out whose energy is whose, so promoting the idea that we're all just reflections will make sorting through life and finding independence even more challenging.

You create your own reality.

This is one that I fully believe in…to a point. It's true that the power of your thoughts can completely alter your life in the best possible way, but you have to remember that you're

33

building a new reality in a world where a million other realities have already been created by others. This means that there's a heavy cultural impact to manifestation.

For example, if you're a straight white male, creating your own desired reality on top of a reality that is already built for you (patriarchal America) isn't too much of a stretch. On the other hand, if you're a queer black woman and a single mom, you are trying to create a reality which goes against the cultural realities that were built to prevent you from building your own, making it that much harder.

Racism and sexism are rampant in this distortion. When you've successfully created your own reality, it may be a result of pure magic, or it may be a result of privilege. And it's most likely a combination.

Good vibes only!

34

"Don't give any attention to the negative news, because then you'll be feeding the negativity and making it worse. Focus on love and light instead. Good vibes only!"

This is a really convenient way to ignore reality and enable oppression. If you focus exclusively on the good, you are not helping innocent people who are hurting. That's like seeing someone getting beat up in the street and thinking, *I'm going to ignore this and focus on love and light for the world instead!* Your focusing on the positive did not save that person. Your focusing on the positive did not change the mind of the person doing the beating. Tell me...what *did* you accomplish?

It's especially important for empaths to understand the consequences of this distortion. Since empaths are so well-acquainted with the pain and suffering of humanity, encouraging this idea would be encouraging the suppression of half of their experience. Saying "Good vibes only!" to an empath is like saying, "Only half of you is allowed here!"

All these new age distortions employ *spiritual bypassing*, which encourages people to bypass their own pain and individual experiences, and results in a world full of people who pretend to be happy because they *should*, not because they *are*.

To be fair, most new age platitudes have the potential to be really life changing and powerful when used correctly. Most people miss the mark, though, especially at the beginning of their spiritual journeys. We'd like to think that these things are much easier than they are, which is completely understandable. How amazing would it be if it was just that simple and easy?

Using these platitudes is like jumping off a cliff. In theory, the potential for these concepts should make me fly when I jump. *I've got magic on my side! I can fly!* But my own personal pain manifests as heavy weights strapped to my ankles. Sure, creating my own reality can give me wings to fly, but unless I recognize and remove the weights that are strapped on to me, I'm going to fall. My wings are useless if they can't carry my baggage.

The baggage that would keep us from flying includes the things we'd like to ignore in favor of the light: our childhood pain, our abuses, our victimhood, our unkind emotions. If we don't realize the finer points and physics of spiritual cliff jumping, like the very real weight of our emotional baggage, flying is much less of a possibility.

What is the baggage that might keep you from flying? In the Do the Work section of this chapter, you'll explore your own experience with these new age concepts and examine where you've gotten stuck.

35

Meet Your Shadows: Victims and Villains

To begin working with your shadow self, you need to know what it's like and what it wants. To make it easier, when we first start examining the shadow, I like to split the shadow self into two roles: the victim and the villain.

The victim (or innocent) is made up of all the bad things that other people have done to you. The villain is made up of all the bad things that you have done to other people. They both have unique reactions to things, and they both want to rise up within you and act on their impulses. Between the two of them, they can make up most of the undesirable traits you have. By personifying your own victim and villain, you will connect to a source of secrets and knowledge that you didn't have access to before.

Who is your victim? What do they look like? How old are they? What are their habits? What are the things they most often talk about? What have people done to you in your life to create this character? What about your villain? What kind of games does your villain like to play? What have you done to others in your life to create this character? When personifying your victim and villain, you're revealing real characters that live inside of you.

When Rose was asked to personify her victim, she noticed that it was a much younger version of her. This younger version of herself always kept her head down and mumbled to herself softly. Rose was sexually abused at a fairly young age, and was conditioned into thinking she would always be in a place of powerlessness.

As a result, her victim tries to find situations in adulthood where she can willingly give up her power, especially sexually. Her family wasn't there for her in times of emotional struggle, so her victim believes that no one will ever support her. This

36

belief drives her to give up on relationships prematurely, because she believes they will never support her. Rose complains about her job constantly and how unfairly they treat her, because she was treated unfairly when she was younger and her victim wants to hold on to that. She's able to find her victimhood in nearly every situation, because more than anything else, her victim wants to be seen. She wants attention and validation, and because she's not receiving it in a positive, loving way, she acts out by finding opportunities to give her power away in a last-ditch effort for attention.

Rose's villain, on the other hand, refuses to be a victim. She guards herself against situations where she might have to be emotionally vulnerable and cuts people out of her life harshly. When she feels slighted by someone, she chooses the path of spite and revenge. She enjoys seducing men she doesn't even care for, just so she can feel her power over them. She revels in that power and manipulation, and she laughs at their loss of control.

37

The victim and villain may seem like complete opposites, but that's usually how they reveal themselves. When it comes to self-growth and exploration, if you've found yourself in a contradiction, you've likely stumbled into truth. The victim and the villain feed and encourage one another. There is not one without the other. The villain usually becomes a villain after being a victim first. Your villain's primary job is actually to prevent you from ever becoming that victim again. And your victim's primary job is to get the attention they didn't get before, by any means necessary, and to hold onto the purity and innocence they had right before the bad things happened to them.

You might see these examples and think, *Those sound horrible! Who would want to be in touch with that?* But this is where it gets really interesting. Think about your favorite television shows, movies, and books. Think about the innocents and the villains you get to know. Personally, my favorite kinds of stories are the ones where the villains can cross over into innocents occasionally, and the innocents can cross over into villains occasionally. When the villain constantly does evil things without any variety, it gets boring. When the innocent constantly does innocent things without any variety, it gets boring. It is so heartwarming and exciting when the villain shows some self-growth and does something kind, and at the same time, it's so satisfying to see the innocent delve into their own villainous destructive tendencies. It's more exciting because it more accurately portrays how people really are. It's more exciting because that's where we see character development and growth.

When you willingly look into your own shadow, your own victim gets to step up into empowerment, and you get to see that. Your own villain gets to expand into kindness, and you get to see that. Your own innocent self gets to descend into some interesting debauchery, and you get to see that too. In this way, it's *so* much more fun to deal with all the different aspects of yourself, and your shadow makes this experience of life a million times more interesting.

The best part? When you get to know your victim and your villain, you can let them be a part of your life *without* destroying anything. You can still embody them at times.

For instance, I sometimes ask my partner to hold space for my victim self, and then I allow myself to react to the situation in my victim mentality. When I do this, I'm validating and acknowledging that my victim self is there. I'm expressing her thoughts (even if they are not thoughts I share normally), and because I express that as my victim, it doesn't hurt my relationship with my partner. Once I allow myself to do this, I can then easily see how those are not thoughts I want to operate out of on a regular basis.

The same goes for my villain. My villain is a bit of an evil seductress born of past trauma, but if I'm with a safe intimate partner, I can allow her to come out and play for a little bit. This acknowledges and validates her existence, while also putting her in a safe place to express herself.

How can you express your victim and your villain in your own life? Where can you create some space for those pieces of yourself to come alive? If you have a partner or friend that you trust, maybe you can explore these concepts together so you can create a safe space for one another.

Now, we can't play out *every* victim and villain reaction, because there's no way to do that without hurting someone. In those cases, you can instead turn to creative expression: writing a song about your victim, writing a suspense novel about your villain, painting a picture of them, doing an interpretive dance. The options are endless. This exercise is, of course, a simplification of our shadows, but starting somewhere simple gets us in the habit of separating out energies and describing them accurately.

The more you can personify and validate the experiences of your victim and your villain, the more you will be able to integrate them into yourself. Having a positive relationship with your dark side ensures that your dark side won't creep into every aspect of your life, silently and slowly ruining your relationships. The better you know yourself, the more control you have over the outcomes in your life. If you work with your dark side, you'll have access to an unending well of creativity and healing, but if you ignore or repress your dark side, you will be blocked and unable to create the change in the world that you would like to create.

39

DO THE WORK

First, take a look at new age distortions in your own life. Then I'll teach you a healthy way to witness, validate, and transform your pain.

New Age Distortions

In your journal, write down a few of the new age concepts that you've been exposed to that **should** have made you feel good but didn't. After thinking about your shadow side and how important your darkness is, why do you think those concepts didn't sit right with you?

Pain Alchemy Affirmations

One way to use positive thinking during your shadow work is to use pain alchemy affirmations instead of positive affirmations. Pain alchemy affirmations allow you to first witness and validate your pain, and then shift your pain toward the positive.

To craft a pain alchemy affirmation, you start with a statement that recognizes your pain. "I am hurt by _____." This first sentence's only job is to validate the fact that you feel pain and allow you to name it.

The next sentence of your pain alchemy affirmation begins with "I know that _____." The purpose of this second sentence is to take that named pain and turn it toward your own inner wisdom, which only your pain could reveal. Sunshine and rainbows will not inform your inner wisdom; only the specific pain and shadow of that feeling can enlighten you to its wisdom.

Once you've written them, read them out loud. You will know if it's the right affirmation for you, because when it hits that sweet spot of validation, you will feel an energetic "click" in your bones. You will feel its power.

Don't worry if you don't quite understand how these work. Practice with a few of your negative feelings. Follow the formula of

40

first naming your pain and then turning that pain toward wisdom. They can be as simple and uncomplicated or as eloquent and long-winded as you'd like. The important part is how it feels when you read it out loud.

Here are some examples of crafting pain alchemy affirmations:

Crappy feeling: I'm bombarded by the negative feelings and the pain of others.

Pain alchemy affirmation: I am hurt by the pain and suffering of others. I know that this deep empathy gives me a fuller knowing of the spectrum of life on earth, allows me to be grateful for my own joy and the joy of others, and allows me to feel that joy just as deeply as the pain.

Crappy feeling: I feel unaccepted for my sensitivity.

Pain alchemy affirmation: I am hurt by the disapproval of my sensitivity. I know that my sensitivity is beautiful, and I do not need to change it. It is a vast network of delicate intuitive synapses that begin and end in my heart.

41

Crappy feeling: I'm terrified of being alone.

Pain alchemy affirmation: I am hurt and scared by the idea of being completely alone with myself. I know that to face this fear with courage, to sink into the wild isolation of independence, is to know myself better.

Crappy feeling: I keep ending up in abusive relationships with narcissists.

Pain alchemy affirmation: I am hurt by the pattern of abuse I have found myself in. I know that I am not confined to these patterns, and with honest self-work and self-love, I can break free of these karmic plays.

Crappy feeling: Why am I making myself smaller for other people?

Pain alchemy affirmation: I am hurt by my willingness to make myself smaller to accommodate others' emotional needs. I know that by doing this I'm not truly helping them or myself. My relationships will be stronger and more meaningful when I fully show up as myself.

The goal of pain alchemy affirmations is to literally alchemize your pain into something beautiful and healing. These affirmations can help you use your pain for the purpose of healing, instead of just looking for healing to replace your pain.

Write down a few of your painful feelings, and craft your very own pain alchemy affirmations. Your first goal is to simply validate your feeling, and your second goal is to turn your pain into a healing tool.

Who's Your Victim? Who's Your Villain?

42

In your journal, use a page for your victim and a page for your villain. Write down everything you can about them both. What do they look like? How old are they? What are their habits, their favorite colors, their favorite kind of music? What do they like to wear? For your victim, what have others done to them? For your villain, what have they done to others? Describe each of them in as much detail as you can.

Don't take it too seriously; this is an exercise that can feel oddly fun if you let it. Don't judge yourself for your victim and villain. Look at them like interesting characters, and there's no need to put a positive spin on them.

When you're done, look at your descriptions. These descriptions are of two characters—characters that are like actors dying to get some screen time. How can you validate them without letting them destroy your life? How can you give them attention? What kind of safe expression can you give them? Do you need to embody and channel your victim with a friend? Do you need to write a dark story about your villain? How do they *want* to be seen?

CHAPTER 3

Uncovering
Core
Wounds

The dead bird stiffened in my tiny hands, its gray-blue feathers larger and longer than my six-year-old fingers. It had hit the window of my grandparents' cabin in northern Minnesota. I thought I could save it. I wanted to save it. I'd found a box for it, laid down a towel, put birdseed and water in it, and watched with eager eyes, hoping the injured creature would pull through. At first, it seemed like it might. It tried moving around a bit, and I monitored its breathing.

When my father found out I was harboring the injured chickadee, he was vocal about his disapproval. He told me that it was as good as dead and that I may as well leave it—that this was just how things went. I'm not sure if he was simply having a bad day when I found that bird, because even to this day he supports my Snow White leanings with critters, but on that day, he made me feel stupid. He made me feel stupid for caring about a creature that was likely going to die. I felt rejected, like my compassion and sensitivity were completely out of place in this world. I felt as unseen by my father as that dying little bird did.

The image of its lifeless body in my hands is one that lives on in the hollows of my chest. It was the first time I felt the sting of empathy, and the first time I felt shattering emotional pain. This is my core wound, the one wound that so many other wounds circle back to—the core foundational wound of being unseen and unaccepted as a sensitive being.

Everyone has their own core wounds, but as an empath, discovering your core wound is even more important. Since empaths are so sensitive and highly attuned to emotions, their core wounds can be magnified much more than the average person's. Such intense wounding can create a foundation that's been built on pain, and if your foundation is built on

44

pain, anything you continue to build in your life afterward will have that same wounding running through it. This is why discovering your core wounds and working with them will reset the tone of your foundation and your life.

Your Core Wound

Each of us has our very own dead bird story. Each of us has our own unique core wound, and though the narratives may be unique to each person, they usually share a very common thread.

This common thread is the empath's first experience of feeling like they are too sensitive for this world and that their sensitivity is unwelcome or unseen. When was the first time you remember feeling emotional pain? What's the first memory that comes to mind? There may be a few, but try and focus on the earliest possible memory. How old were you? Who was involved? Where were you?

45

This core wound is an incredibly important foundational event that you've built the structures of your emotional pain upon. In most cases, many of us are building onto this foundation for the entirety of our lives without even realizing that it's all connected and traceable to our childhoods. Our pains can often feel very separate and unrelated to those of us who aren't actively involved in our emotional self-awareness. We fail to see how each new pain is simply further adding to our structure, using those original blueprints of emotional suffering.

Once we can look at our emotional pain structures like an architect might look at a building, understanding the form and function of each piece, we can clearly see the source of our feelings and consequently see where we can break it down to build something better.

A lifetime of struggle because of a dead bird? Seems a little much.

Just as a stone cast into a pond creates ripples much bigger than the stone's initial impact, the same goes for our core wounds. The core wound simply sets the stage, the emotional tonality, and every action after that either affirms or denies that tone. If you had parents and family that understood how to nurture a sensitive child, then perhaps the effects of your core wound were lessened through that nurturing love. For a lot of empaths, though, their families were unable to see and nurture that sensitivity properly. Sometimes people turn to criticism or anger when they don't understand someone's feelings, and that's an extra unfortunate occurrence when those feelings belong to the empath. What starts as a singular foundational wound of being unseen in sensitivity can then snowball into rejection upon rejection that only affirms the painful tone of that wound.

46

"Don't take it so personally."

"You're being dramatic."

"Oh, stop it, you're fine."

"Why can't you just get over it?"

"Don't be mad/sad."

"You need to toughen up to make it in this world."

These are all things the empath often hears growing up from those who can't or won't see and acknowledge their sensitivity. These are all things that confirm the empath's greatest fear: they're too sensitive for this world. Every additional painful experience contributes to the building up of our emotional pain structures.

What is *your* core wound? What is *your* emotional pain foundation?

Retrieving Your Inner Child

Not only do our core wounds create foundations for our pain, but they also cause what's known in shamanic communities as "soul loss." *Soul loss* is what happens when a soul experiences trauma, and a piece of the soul fractures and breaks off to protect itself from the pain of that trauma. The piece of soul that fractures contains a vital energy that is necessary for the wholeness of the human life, and at some point, we all must retrieve these lost pieces. We all experience soul loss many times throughout our lives. It's much more common than one would think. We all have many different pieces that have separated from our bodies from many different stages of life. When soul loss happens, that vital energy stays the same age and mentality it was when it separated from the body.

When I found my inner six-year-old crying over the dead bird, she was still six years old, still insecure about her sensitivity, and still at my grandparents' cabin in northern Minnesota. Your inner child may also be the same age as when you first experienced the wound of sensitivity, in the same place where it first happened. This is especially likely if you have dreams of those places. Our inner lost pieces like to help us out by creating our dreamscape in places where our treasured energies are still hidden, waiting to be recovered.

Those who have experienced prolonged periods of abuse and those who experience dissociation are more likely to have more soul loss than others. This is because soul loss is actually a defensive strategy for the soul, and the more trauma the soul is exposed to, the more it will try to protect itself. It recognizes that something awful is happening, whether it's on a physical, emotional, sexual, or psychological level, and it wants to do everything in its power to protect the soul's vital energy, so it splits off and separates from the painful event.

This is why, when we discover our lost pieces, they're incredibly potent and pure, just as they existed right before or as the trauma happened. While we can't erase the pain and trauma we've endured, we can reclaim those lost pieces and reintegrate their power into ourselves.

The cultural conditioning of "good" feelings versus "bad" feelings makes soul loss even more of an epidemic, because the more we push away or ignore the "bad" parts of us, the more additional soul loss occurs. If you tell parts of yourself that they're not welcome, eventually they'll listen and leave you. As a result, there are times that we can get so comfortable with this soul loss that it almost feels like we've found some level of spiritual peace. Those "bad" pieces are hidden away where they don't have to be dealt with, which can feel like a relief to an overwhelmed empath. While this may work for a while, our repressed pain always finds a way to come up, and the longer we avoid that pain, the more it eats away at us and begins to manipulate us from the shadows.

The best way to retrieve your inner child and lost soul pieces is to work with a trusted shaman or shamanic practitioner. This isn't always a possibility, though, so you can always work on building a relationship with your inner child yourself. At the end of this chapter is a guided meditation to meet and retrieve your inner child.

The most important thing to remember about retrieving your inner child is that they are just that: a child. They remain exactly as you left them, without the love and understanding they truly needed at the time of the soul loss. Because of that, they have specific needs in order to be integrated back into the body. You must treat them as a being separate from yourself, and mother them as if they were your own child. They need to feel safe and loved to be integrated back into your body. You must give them now the love that they needed then.

My own inner child needed to be seen and validated for her sensitivity. She needed to feel like it was okay to care about a dying chickadee. One way I respected her (and myself) was with my willingness to continue caring for injured creatures. From baby bunnies escaping cats to birds hitting windows, I allowed myself to care for the dying, even if it hurt me—all because that initial experience with the chickadee stuck with me. It wasn't until years later that I discovered the spiritual meaning and message of the chickadee: be brave in using your voice and speaking your truth, while knowing that your truth expands across both the positive and the negative, and that they are both equally valid.

Your own inner child carries messages and meanings for you as well. They want to know that you respect them, and finding ways to honor them will show them that you're here to stay. You may even find that, like mine, your core wound may involve a secret message that clues you into your bigger purpose here on Earth.

49

Finding Your Mother Wound

Many empaths have a very deep *mother wound*. A mother wound occurs when, as a sensitive child, you didn't receive the kind of mothering you needed. If your mother was very strict and emotionally withholding, you have a mother wound. If your mother was overly emotional and overbearing, forcing you to take on the mother role as a child, you have a mother wound. If your mother abandoned you or was emotionally absent, you have a mother wound.

As a sensitive empath, your mother wound likely runs deep and affects your relationships as an adult. Until you address that wound, you will find yourself playing out different versions of the same wound in all of your relationships.

The way we approach a mother wound is the same as the way we approach an inner child: we need to give ourselves *now* what we needed then. If your mother didn't nurture your sensitivity, you need to nurture your own sensitivity now. If your mother was absent in your darkest hours, you need to show up for yourself now. You need to learn how to mother yourself. Even if your core wounds aren't directly related to your mother, the ability to mother yourself in your core wounds is paramount.

Learning how to mother yourself isn't easy, and more than that, it can feel incredibly unfair. There's a part of you that wants to rage against the idea of mothering yourself, because you know that you *deserved* a mother who could love you the way you needed to be loved. You did deserve one, and you deserve one now. I wish I could say that you will find that in another person or that your real mother will grow into exactly what you need, but sometimes that never happens. Sometimes we never find another human being to fill that mothering role. You're right; it's totally unfair. Like any other emotion, that feeling of injustice needs to be seen and validated. But then, it's time to step up and mother yourself.

The easiest way to begin mothering yourself is to start with the basics. When you are feeling the urge to collapse into your mother's arms, and those arms are nowhere to be found, you can start small. Turn inward and ask yourself, *How can I take care of myself right now?*

It could start with drinking a glass of water, eating a good meal, taking a nap, even taking a shower. Any step you can take in the direction of providing for your own needs is a step toward mothering yourself. The more you take these smaller steps, the more you'll be able to take larger ones. You can ask yourself, *What would I want my mother to say to me right now?*

and write yourself a letter, telling yourself exactly what you need.

Another way to heal the mother wound is to turn to God. Whether you are a follower of the Goddess, Gaia, Christianity, or anything else, you can turn to a Divine Mother to help you. Your biological parents on this earth are not your true parents. You are a child of God, of Nature, and your truest parents are figures and forces of divinity. If you can turn to a Divine Mother for mothering when your human mother cannot help you, she will help you find your footing, and that Divine Mother will flourish inside of you.

Keira had a very absent mother growing up. When her mother was gone, her two sisters were there with her. One of her sisters was incredibly mean to her, bullying her emotionally and physically to a degree that was completely traumatizing. She felt betrayed by her mother, who allowed it to happen, she felt betrayed by her sister, who intentionally hurt her, and she felt betrayed by her other sister, who watched it happen and did nothing.

51

When Keira came to me for a soul retrieval, she talked a lot about a group of friends, all women, that she recently lost due to betrayal. One woman victimized and bullied her, while the others allowed it to happen. Keira didn't realize it at the time, but she was playing out old patterns from her childhood and reliving her mother wound in her adult relationships.

When she made that connection, I had her tell herself all of the things she wished her friends would tell her, and everything she said perfectly mirrored what she wished she would have felt and heard from her mother and her sisters. When she started delving into mothering herself, she turned to the Goddess Lilith for support, a deity she already had a close relationship with.

Mothering Your Inner Child

The process of coaxing your inner child back to you can be incredibly emotional. Convincing them that they're safe now and that you will take care of them will bring up all the painful feelings that caused the separation in the first place. They need to be seen in that pain and then loved just the same. By telling them that they're safe, you're also telling yourself that you are safe as well. Don't be surprised if you have the overwhelming urge to weep when you truly connect with your inner child. Allow yourself to feel whatever emotions come up for you and for your inner child.

This kind of self-work is heavy as hell. Getting your inner child to come back is only one piece of the puzzle. Another piece is convincing them to stay and allowing them to fully integrate into you, which can take some time after the initial retrieval. Doing this can be painful and uncomfortable, and we need *something* to temper all this heaviness. That *something* is joy.

The key to fully integrating and mothering your inner child is joy. Children need to experience joy in order to learn and evolve in their environments. You will have to get to know your inner child and find out what they need to stay with you. Finding out what your inner child needs is as unique a process as getting to know a new friend.

Establishing a relationship with them is a necessity, and being able to ask them questions will make all the difference. They'll want you to do childlike activities with them, things they enjoyed or things they wanted to do at the time of the soul loss. What do they like to do? Do they like to color? Buy a brand new coloring book and pencils. Do they like to dance? Dance! Do they like to play mermaids? Take them to the beach. Is their favorite color yellow? Work some yellow into your wardrobe. Is their favorite food spaghetti? Looks like you're having spaghetti for dinner! Whatever you can do that celebrates their personality, their sensitivity, and their existence will not only fully integrate them, but it will also bring childlike joy back to you in full force.

Every inner child is different. One of my clients was a woman who grew up as a tomboy and later enlisted in the military. A condition of her inner child was to be able to feel more feminine and do more feminine things. She felt a bit smothered by her masculine sense of duty and order, and wanted to feel free to be both masculine and feminine. For my client, this meant she would allow herself to dress up, do her hair and makeup, and have dance parties with her girlfriends. Doing these things didn't mean that she had to change herself to be traditionally feminine all the time, but it allowed her to experience something her inner child desperately wanted, which anchored and integrated her inner child into her.

Another client of mine was a man whose inner child felt an oppressive need to be intelligent, which made him feel like he couldn't enjoy learning for the sake of learning when he was young. At that age, he was diagnosed with a learning disability, which made him feel like he had to prove his intelligence to his family and teachers at every turn. During his session, his inner child came up to me out of curiosity and wanted to be involved in the energy healing I was doing. His requirement to stay was simply to be able to learn new things for the sake of curiosity and fun, without any added pressure to it, and without worrying whether other people thought he was smart or not.

My own inner child is an animal lover, so part of our deal for her to stay was for me to get a puppy. That puppy ended up being the most healing creature in the entire world for her and for me. We played with him, we cared for him, we snuggled with him. Unfortunately, he was not in this world for very

53

long, but the time we spent with him anchored my inner child within me forever. I can also admit that once she was integrated within me, I naturally took myself less seriously and worked more fun and amusement into my life. Since I work primarily in the shadows, that amusement is absolutely essential for this work to be successful and sustainable for me.

What are the conditions of your own inner child? What do they need in order to stay with you? Working with your inner child can be like negotiating a spiritual contract, and you have to make sure you can give them what they really need. Ask them what makes them happy, and do your best to provide that for them. How can you mother them? Knowing how to bring your inner child joy is what will anchor them in you forever.

Joy is the most potent force of manifestation magic available, so you will find that the transformation and alchemy available to you when you embrace your childlike joy is overwhelmingly powerful. This kind of joy is especially powerful because it comes out of the acknowledgment and validation of emotional pain, and that is an empath superpower.

It takes time to heal the mother wound, but reframing the thought of *I don't have a mother to help me* to *How can I mother myself?* can accelerate that healing.

I am still constantly working with my own mother wound, learning and relearning how to mother myself and take care of myself. Maybe you're still constantly working with your own mother wound, or maybe you're just starting. It's a long process for any empath, and it involves a lot of trial and error and a lot of communication with the self. It remains a bittersweet practice, always mourning the loss of the love you needed while gaining the strength to provide it for yourself. Working with the mother wound builds a strange foundation within you, one that surprises you in its depth and capability, and one that

54

consistently teaches you how to be a powerful and independent human being.

DO THE WORK

Now it's your turn to find your core wound and inner child. Although this process can be hard, it can also lead you to deep healing and help you reclaim lost power.

Remembering Your Core Wound

When was the first time you remember feeling emotional pain? Sink into that memory. What was the situation? Where were you? How old were you? Describe the experience in your journal. Use as many of your senses as you can. What do you see? Hear? Smell? Taste? Feel? You may have more than one memory, and that's okay. You can journal about each experience, since each one will be tied to a piece of yourself that you need to retrieve. Try to start with your earliest memory, though—that's where the foundational wound will be.

55

Inner Child Retrieval

Find a comfortable space where you won't be disturbed. Turn off your phone and prepare your space. Feel free to burn sage, light candles or incense, do a few rituals or prayers. Play some music in the background. Shamanic drumming works best, but whatever music relaxes you is okay too.

Sit comfortably or lie down, whichever feels best to you. Start with a few minutes of deep breathing, inhaling through the nose, exhaling through the mouth. When you feel your body relaxing, think back to the time and place of your core wound. Visualize yourself stepping through a clear barrier, like a sheet of glass or a gentle waterfall, into this place. You are stepping into another world and another time. You have entered the place where your inner child is.

Allow yourself time to let the environment form around you. Explore it if you wish. It may look exactly how it did at the time of your core wound, but it might look a little different. Notice how it feels to be there.

Now you're going to find your inner child. They might come right up to you; they might be hiding from you. When you find them, they could be in any emotional state. They might be smiling and happy to see you. They might be cowering and hiding in a corner from the trauma they experienced. They could be angry with you. In whatever way they appear, be gentle and patient with them.

Spend a few minutes simply connecting with them and letting them get used to your presence. You'll find that you'll understand what they want to say to you without them actually saying it. Without any judgment, let them tell you how they feel, and when they finish, explain to them your side of the story. Tell them that you want to take care of them and that they're safe. They may resist you at first. You may have to lovingly convince them. But hold the connection with your pure intention until you're both at an understanding and they feel comfortable enough to come back with you. Ask them what they'll need to be happy and to stay with you, and genuinely promise that you will give it to them. More than anything, make them feel seen and appreciated.

When you're out of the meditation, journal about your experience. Now is the time to start fulfilling your promise to them. What did they say they needed in order to stay with you? What did they say they liked? You can go into quiet meditation to ask them questions at any time. It's good to check in with them often and make sure the connection is strong.

Follow through on your promises. Do the things they wanted to do. Get a coloring book. Cook their favorite food. Take them to the beach. Wear their favorite color. Get a pet. Do the things that bring them joy. Your inner child won't stay with you unless you can prove that you are a safe and fun place for them.

CHAPTER 4

Mastering Emotional Energy

I began personifying my feelings even before I knew what I was doing or why. Since I had so many painful feelings when I was younger, I had to journal about them to feel like I could handle them. There was no one to talk to. Sometimes journaling and personifying my feelings helped a lot, sometimes only a little. But I kept doing it because it was the only thing I could think of to do. Time and time again, I wrote down my feelings—my heartache, my depression, my hope, my longing.

As time went on and some of the same feelings visited me over and over again, my writing became more descriptive and poetic. I could no longer call upon them only by name. They demanded more space to breathe. They demanded a proper introduction. The same feelings started forming into their own people with their own personalities and quirks.

Pain became a beautiful woman with eyelashes of needles. She knew she was beautiful, and she wanted to draw people close to her, but she felt like she could only hurt others. She knew that if she ever kissed another, her eyelashes would scrape against their skin. Depression became a used paint palette of blues and yellows muddied together. She was an artist with a macabre sense of wit, and she liked to paint van Gogh replicas while listening to Billie Holiday croon "Gloomy Sunday" on repeat.

Every feeling had a story, a collection of different characters taking their turn on the stage of my life. They became almost like imaginary friends, though they were nothing close to imaginary. They were living feelings inside of me, revealing themselves to me in intimate and powerful ways.

Little did I know at the time, I had taught myself one of the most helpful techniques for identifying energy, one that I still use today.

Feeling all the emotions all the time can make life as an empath incredibly confusing. It can be hard to sort through all of your emotions, especially since we were taught as children that there are "good" and "bad" emotions. Dividing our emotions into "good" and "bad" makes the empath experience even more painful, since we're forced to distance ourselves from the "bad" in a way that doesn't empower our emotional process. Ultimately, this disconnection makes it so we can't even identify what our feelings are or what to do with them. By realizing that every emotion is an energy, and every energy is unique, like a signature, you can identify, personify, and use each and every emotion for your own empowerment and strength.

Feelings Are Energy, Energies Have Signatures, Signatures Are Unique

Journaling extensively about all my feelings gave me a deep knowing of how and when each feeling came up. I became well acquainted with my painful emotions, and in the process, each emotion developed its own unique *energy signature*. An energy signature is like a designated bar code for each feeling, and once you know that bar code, you can identify and work with it easily.

Energy signatures are different for each person. My energy signature for anxiety may be completely different from yours, based on each of our personal experiences and intuition. While my Depression might be a witty macabre artist, yours might be someone else entirely. Mine might not feel the same as yours, but if you know exactly how yours feels, you'll always be able to differentiate between your feelings and the feelings of other people.

It's easy to begin identifying an energy signature. When you're experiencing a strong feeling, sit quietly with that feeling and visualize it. Allow an image to take shape. Use your intuitive senses to describe that feeling and that image as thoroughly as you can. What color is it? What shape? Does it have a smell, a feel? How does it move and where does it sit in your body? Develop that picture of your feeling as much as you can. If you're feeling strong in the connection, ask it questions. Is it anger? Is it grief? What is it exactly? Is it a person, and if it is, what is their name? What do they like or dislike? The deeper you go with it in the beginning, the easier it will be to recognize later. You're not only putting a visual to it but also strengthening your connection to the actual energy it represents. You are essentially putting a name tag on that energy so it will be easier for you to identify in a crowd of other energies.

If you've had any trouble witnessing or validating your feelings in the past, this is by far the easiest way to start. Maybe you've had the experience where you've been completely overwhelmed by feelings and you weren't even sure which feelings were yours. It may sound counterintuitive to try to describe the details of a feeling when you can't even name what the feeling is, but by picking out the smaller details in a feeling using creative visualization, even among a slew of different feelings, you will slowly build upon those details to create one unmistakable feeling. Once you know those feelings creatively, you'll be able to communicate with them. Each feeling has its own message for you, but they can't communicate their message if you haven't given them the space to exist and expand.

When Vanessa told me she was feeling a lump of anxiety in her throat, we decided to acquaint ourselves with it. I asked her to describe how it felt and what it looked like. I asked her to give it a name. As it turns out, Vanessa's anxiety was an old woman named Pearl.

Pearl was a sassy broad with her handbag clutched closely to her chest, and she had no fear of expressing herself. Pearl was nervous about the safety of her material things, like the car Vanessa parked down the street, and whether Vanessa locked her apartment, and whether other people were touching her things. When we asked Pearl why her material things were so important, she said, "Because I didn't have them before this."

When Vanessa grew up, she went through a period in her life where her family had next to nothing in terms of material things. Her mother had moved them into a house in a nice neighborhood so they could attend a good school, which took all the money she had. They bought plastic lawn furniture for their living room, since they couldn't afford traditional sofas at the time. When money began flowing again, her mother emphasized the importance of choosing quality pieces that gave her a sense of pride and accomplishment for her life.

61

As a result, Vanessa had a unique relationship to her material things, one that emphasized their importance and her pride in nice things. So when her anxiety came up, it was really Pearl, reminding her of her connection to those material things and her fear of losing them. The more we talked to Pearl and listened to what she said, the less anxious she became. She began to settle into the role of a guide, giving Vanessa all sorts of helpful, albeit sassy as hell, advice. By personifying her negative feeling of anxiety, Vanessa was able to turn that feeling into a learning tool and a helpful guide—one that hilariously called her out when she needed it (like when Pearl scolded her for not drinking her green juice.)

Sometimes our energy signatures aren't as flexible in their expressions and how they communicate with us. Sometimes negative feelings want to stay negative, and there's not much that we can do to change their mind. Anxiety in the form of panic is a good example. Panic is such a raw and hyperadrenalized emotion that it will continue to operate at that same panicked vibration, and working with it is more about subduing it and making sure it doesn't rule your life, rather than hoping it will turn into something else. In that case, your energy signature for panic might be a large man running around your house, screaming and knocking furniture over and things off shelves, breaking everything and refusing to actually talk to you.

Building energetic signatures is like discovering little gremlins that have been living in your body for years. Some of them are sassy old ladies who just want to give you practical advice, and some of them are mischievous little jerks who just want to cause trouble. Each feeling is tied to a character of sorts. You'll have the opportunity to start building on your energy signatures in the Do the Work section. When you get to know these characters, your experience of your emotions becomes a story in itself, and not just a negative feeling. And once you know these characters well, you'll always be able to recognize and work with them in a productive way.

The Binary Bind of "Good" and "Bad" Feelings

Feelings are tricky little beasts. They encompass the whole spectrum of life experience, and it can be incredibly difficult to make sense of them all. Humans have developed a way to make all of this a little bit easier: we've divided emotions into "good" feelings and "bad" feelings. Joy, happiness, excitement, peace, and love are all "good" emotions, while depression, anxiety, jealousy, and anger are all "bad" emotions.

From a very early age, children are taught that the "good" feelings are what we aim for and are positively reinforced, while the "bad" emotions are undesired and are negatively reinforced. As a result, children develop very binary emotional landscapes that don't leave a lot of space for actually feeling without judging what they are feeling. The more that landscape is enforced, both externally and internally, the more that child develops into a repressed adult with unbalanced empathy. And this happens with everyone to some degree. No one is an exception to this.

The consequences of binary emotional landscapes are even greater for the born empath. Since the very nature of empathy is to feel everything, and since pain is often felt more intensely than joy, the empath learns that at least half of their entire nature is undesirable and unacceptable. This sets them up for a lifetime of secrecy and shame.

As a result, many empaths naturally gravitate toward lives in spiritual communities as a way to cope with their struggles. The trend of the positive thinking movement that's rampant in spiritual communities, however, can potentially cause more harm than help for an empath with a conditioned binary emotional landscape. The positive thinking movement overemphasizes the glorification of "good" feelings as a replacement for feeling the "bad" ones and reinforces the notion that if you feel the "bad" emotions, you're not a "good" spiritual person.

When in the very beginning stages of realizing my emotional pain, I saw a series of healers for treatments in my spiritual development. Some pretty heavy feelings were coming up around some pretty serious themes like rape, eating disorders, and abuse, and I could feel them bubbling up just underneath the surface, waiting to be seen and exorcised.

As I would begin to express these feelings to my healers, they would tell me that I didn't have to talk about them. They told me that merely talking about them would bring attention to them and feed the negativity. As I received these sessions, I could feel the energy they were using on me. They were all gifted healers with the best of intentions, and the healing energy was fantastic, but I found that the energy couldn't land. It couldn't fully integrate into my body. Now I know that it couldn't integrate because the places that really needed the healing energy were intentionally closed off.

Maybe you've experienced the same thing in your own spiritual journey. Maybe you've experienced some wonderful energy from healers or teachers that never seemed to stick with you. Have you ever felt like, as much as you've tried, you couldn't get fully on board with positive thinking? Were there certain things that were said that didn't sit well with you, or made you feel secretly ashamed of how much you felt all the time? Do you feel like only half of you can show up to positive thinking because of all the hidden feelings you have from your own binary emotional landscape? This is an indication that you need more than positive thinking. You need to be able to feel all of your feelings, even the "bad" feelings. Until you can feel all of them without shame, the "good" stuff won't be able to fully integrate into your body.

This doesn't mean that the positive thinking movement is all bad. Alas, that would be yet another binary way of thinking, and the binary is never fully true. While it's not all bad, it's not all good either. Like most things, it's how we can use it for our wholeness rather than our divisiveness that makes it productive. Many spiritual seekers want to bathe in the goodness of it, because they initially search for spirituality to take away their pain. This is how we end up with a handful of happy-Zen-healer folks who seem like they've got it all figured out when, in reality, their spirituality is shallow because they won't acknowledge or entertain the "bad" pieces of themselves. Our core wounds are generally put into the "bad" category, which then furthers the divide between us and our emotional growth. Integrating your "bad" humanness into your positive divineness is the surest way to be the fullest expression of yourself, especially as an empath.

I think it's important to remember that we're all, without exception, sparkly divine mystical beings with the entire power of the universe at our fingertips. I think it's equally as important to remember that we're all, without exception, these weird human creatures that fart, make bad decisions, and feel insecure. And it's even more important to remember that the latter does not negate the former.

Sacred, Harmful, and Neutral Emotional Messages

Despite what we've been taught about binary emotional landscapes, no emotion is truly all "bad" or all "good." There are positive and negative things found in each feeling. If you can tune into your own emotions and identify their unique energy signatures, you'll be able to use each one for your healing.

Instead of dividing up your emotions into "bad" and "good" columns, let's instead take each emotion and divide it into three categories: the sacred, the harmful, and the neutral. Every single feeling can manifest in those three ways, and once you've identified the energy signatures of each of those feelings, you can discover what those feelings need from you and how to express them using those three categories.

Every experience and feeling can be turned into a transformative one, which is the sacred manifestation of that feeling. Out of your pain, you can learn truth, wisdom, beauty, and love. Sacred expression of emotions is always a reclamation of something: your power, your independence, your creativity.

It's easy to take a "good" emotion and use it as a sacred expression. This is when you feel compassion and volunteer at a homeless organization. This is when you feel generous and donate money to a cause you believe in. This is when you feel selfless and help out your friends and family.

It's much harder to take a "bad" emotion and use it as a sacred expression. This takes intention and practice, and to begin, you need to turn to your energy signatures. Once you've built up your energy signature for that "bad" emotion, it's much easier to communicate with it and understand what its message is and what it needs from you. And when you're fully conscious of the feeling you're experiencing and what it's communicating, it's easier to consciously choose how to react and express it. When you're feeling angry, if you first sink into the feeling and allow yourself to recognize and build upon the energy signature, you can then choose to channel that anger into an activity which transmutes that feeling into something that heals. For example, if you have just experienced sexism at your job and you're raging about it, you could turn that anger into an article about sexism that opens people's eyes. You could use that rage to fuel a vigorous hike you've been putting off. You could use that rage to organize a feminist group at your job. If you're communicating with that energy signature, it will tell you what it needs to do. When you're feeling jealous, maybe what that emotion needs is for you to plan a trip and fulfill something on your bucket list. Every "bad" emotion has a job that can create good, and opening up that line of communication is how to create a sacred manifestation of it.

The harmful manifestations of emotions are what most of us are accustomed to. This is when you're cruel to other people or yourself as a result of your feelings. It usually happens when you're simply not aware of any other options. It's not your fault; you've been raised to believe that there are only good feelings and bad feelings, so your brain is already wired to avoid your bad feelings. The longer you avoid those feelings, the more those feelings give speed to the harmful manifestations. Many times, we won't be able to turn toward the sacred manifestations until we realize we've wandered into the harmful territory.

It's important to realize that even "good" emotions can have harmful manifestations. For example, maybe your happiness in your new relationship affects how you communicate with your friends and family. Maybe you aren't able to see what your loved ones need because of your new rose-colored glasses, or you're simply refusing to see because you don't want them to affect your happiness. This is another reminder that "good" and "bad" emotions aren't that simple, and that knowing your energy signatures for your "good" feelings are just as important.

Neutral manifestations of emotion are the hardest to work with. It's usually not until you've delved into the sacred manifestations for a while that neutrality becomes easier. This happens when you experience an emotion and realize that it doesn't need an expression. This is when the toddler cries out to Mom, and Mom can simply acknowledge the child and say, "Yes, I see!" These are the feelings you can see and validate, and that's all they need from you. When you make a habit of allowing your feelings the space for sacred expression, your feelings begin to shift, and you'll need those expressions less and less until they become neutral. Having a neutral reaction to your emotion is similar to watching an annoying commercial on television. You don't like it, it annoys or disturbs you in some way, but once you've seen it and it's over, it really doesn't

67

matter anymore. Neutrality is like the master class of emotional expression, and as such, it's best to focus on the practice of sacred manifestation until you've been working with your energy signatures for a while. In the Do the Work section, you'll have the opportunity to work with your energy signatures and their sacred, harmful, and neutral expressions.

The Pleasures of a Pity Party

"Don't feel sorry for yourself" is something you've probably told yourself multiple times. You've probably heard it in one form or another from friends and family too. They usually add, "It could be worse!" or "At least you don't have it as bad as Kathy!"

In theory, those are the ways we shift our focus from feeling sorry for ourselves to feeling grateful for what we have. If you think about it, though, the fact that there are starving children around the world is not going to make you more grateful for your abusive relationship with your boyfriend. Sure, you might feel more grateful for the food on your table because of it, and that's a wonderful thing, but how is that going to help you with your boyfriend? And who cares about how bad Kathy has it if that has nothing to do with what you're actually facing?

Just because other people have things worse than you doesn't mean your problem isn't valid. Gratitude is an incredibly beautiful tool and practice, but you don't *have* to feel grateful for your problems. Forcing yourself to feel grateful for the things you want to change isn't going to actually create the change you want.

Self-pity is an emotion that comes around for a very specific reason.

68

Self-pity says, "You are not listening to me or validating me."

Self-pity wants you to slow down and process the experiences you've lived through.

If you refuse to process your own self-pity and victimhood, it will undoubtedly build up inside of you, seeping out into the rest of your life. You may feel slighted by others over and over again, all because you weren't able to process your self-pity from something that happened years ago.

I say throw a pity party! Throw yourself a conscious, intentional pity party just for your inner victim. For a specified amount of time, usually just a day or an evening at a time, let yourself be as sorry for yourself as you possibly can. Sink into those feelings. Journal about how awful people have been to you without trying to correct yourself or make yourself more positive. Vent about anything and everything to a friend, as long as they agree not to steer you toward positivity. Be bitter. Eat tons of junk food. Watch Netflix in between bouts of crying and swearing and venting. You may be surprised by how good it feels to simply allow yourself to feel terrible without trying to change it.

You've been a victim. Part of you is still a victim. You get to own that part too. When you've truly validated your victimhood and your self-pity, you'll find that it naturally goes away on its own and reveals the deeper emotions you haven't been able to work with yet. Owning the feeling of self-pity and letting it happen naturally takes away the desperate urge to not come off as a victim, which removes the barrier in your ability to work with your deeper feelings.

The secret to the pity party is that you're not only processing your self-pity. Your self-pity is just a mask that ties together the negative feelings you have that you haven't been able to

69

express. You may find that once you make space for your self-pity, those other emotions that you've been pushing away will rise up again. You may feel your deep-rooted sadness or anger. You may feel suppressed trauma forming a lump in your throat. This is totally normal. The thing about self-pity is that it can't exist as an emotion by itself; self-pity is just a knot of tangled "bad" emotions that haven't been allowed to express themselves. By creating the space for shame-free self-pity, you're also creating the space for shame-free emotional expression in general, and that knot of "bad" feelings needs that space to untangle itself.

If one pity party isn't enough to process those feelings, keep going. Schedule another pity party. Try a few different methods to let yourself feel it. It's okay if it takes a while. I've had an intentional pity party that lasted two whole weeks. They were miserable, lazy weeks, but at the end, I had processed an enormous amount of self-pity and the deeper emotions underneath that spanned a couple of years. Once processed, I noticed that those same themes which had plagued me before no longer had the power to seep into my life.

Throwing yourself an intentional pity party is oddly and incredibly empowering! If you and a friend are both going through this process, you could try making it a group party! You'll be able to plan a pity party for yourself when you Do the Work below.

As a rule, if an emotion keeps surfacing, especially self-pity, it's because you still need to go deep into it.

The Importance of Clearing Practices

As an empath, you are incredibly sensitive to energy. And anytime you work with your emotions, you literally move and

70

transmute tons of energy. This is why it's so important to have effective clearing practices. *Clearing practices* ensure that your aura, as well as the physical space you inhabit, is clean and clear of any stagnant or excess energy that is hanging around. Clearing the energy is important both for you and anyone else around you, so no one gets stuck in or reabsorbs the energy you've been working with. Refer to Energetic Clearing Tools in the resources section for suggestions on how to do this.

DO THE WORK

Mastering emotional energy takes practice, and that practice requires taking a first step. These exercises will help you take that crucial first step.

Your Emotional Messages

You're going to build an energy signature. Pick an emotion, preferably one of your negative emotions that comes up frequently. Allow yourself to sink into that feeling. Breathe deeply, close your eyes, and experience the energy of that feeling. Using your journal, describe that emotion. What color is it? What does it look like? Is there a smell? A taste? What images do you see? Is it a person? An object? Let that feeling become a personality, someone that you can get to know. It's important to be honest about what you're feeling, since that will create the most accurate energy signature.

Once you've built up a description of your feeling and can start to recognize the energy signature, you can communicate with it. Does that feeling have a name? What does that feeling want? What does it need?

Then brainstorm some ways in which that emotion is manifested. How do you express that emotion in a harmful way? Do you lash out? Do you shut people out? What about your sacred expressions of that emotion? What are some ways that you can give that emotion space in a sacred way? Can you write a blog? Can you take a self-defense class? Can you talk to a friend?

Lastly, what is the message that this emotion is trying to give you? It's okay if you don't know what it is right away. Sometimes you need to work with an energy signature for a while before you can understand its personal message to you.

Here are two examples of my own energy signatures. Yours may be completely different from mine, and you might have a completely different way of describing them. (I really like to play into the drama and poetry of it, but that doesn't mean that you have to do it the same way I do.)

Rage

Rage is bright red. It's the hot poker that's been sitting in the flames, ready to threaten any person who merely looks at me the wrong way. My fire is an unending force to keep that poker glowing red-orange. It's the Goddess Kali, the goddess of death, destruction, and rebirth, the goddess that protects abused women and takes revenge on the abusers, the goddess who wears a necklace of severed heads and a belt of severed arms. Rage feels sharp and angled, but sexy, like the precise edges of expertly applied red lipstick. Rage sits low in the gut and rises to the throat.

Sacred rage is an empowered feminist rant. A strongly worded blog against injustice. A protest. A fight back after being powerless for so long. A cathartic workout that gets the sweat pouring out. A manifesto of truth above all the crap. Unapologetic sass in the face of condemnation. A vent to a compassionate friend.

Harmful rage is taking out my frustration on other people. It's yelling at my partner because of something that happened at work. It's turning my rage inward toward self-destructive tendencies. It's rude and patronizing. It's senseless violence. It doesn't serve anyone or anything; it only wants to destroy.

Rage sends the message that my boundaries (or the boundaries of my loved ones) have been crossed or disrespected. Rage sends the message that active change is required to rectify the situation.

Sadness

Sadness is a dark gray-blue, like the color of the ocean on a gloomy day. Sometimes it's all consuming, like the tide rushing in during a hurricane. Other times, it's calmly in the background, like still waters disappearing on the horizon. It's an ache in my chest, slowly flooding my heart until I have no choice but to empty it out through my tears. Sadness lives in the heart chakra.

Sacred sadness is pure beauty and art. A melody composed through tears. A poem about the experience of life that is painstakingly lovely and honest. A philosophy book. An expression of selfhood that is truly transcendent.

Harmful sadness is perpetual drowning. It's hitting the snooze button on my alarm twelve times too many. It's watching too many sad movies and listening to too many sad songs. It's the slow sink into depression.

Sadness sends the message that I've seen too much and my sensitivities have been activated. It warns me that my attention is required so sadness doesn't slip too far into depression, and it wants me to deal with the less-than-perfect realities I've seen.

You'll want to revisit your energy signatures often. You'll work with these energies for the rest of your life, so it's natural that they'll shift and change as you shift and change. Feel free to revise your energy signatures as they change for you.

Plan for a Pity Party

1. **Clear your schedule.**

    To plan for a pity party, clear some time in your schedule. Decide on a date and time, and how long you will give yourself. I recommend starting with one evening or one day.

2. **Have support available.**

    Deeply emotional and psychological self-work is no
    joke. It's big and it's real, and sometimes you need
    support when going through it. Sometimes the waves
    of emotional instability that are inevitable with chang-
    ing your patterns can feel too overwhelming to handle
    on your own. You want to have someone in your corner
    who knows what you're doing. This could be a trusted
    friend or family member. Know who you can call when
    things get difficult. Know who is strong enough to
    hold space for you without discouraging your work.
    Do you have a friend who is going through this same
    thing? Maybe that person will be with you, or maybe
    they'll be available in case you need to call them. Have
    you started a book club with this process so you have
    a group that is experiencing these challenges together?
    You may not need their support, but having support at
    the ready is always a good idea. Maybe your support is
    a healer or coach or therapist. No matter who it is, they
    need to understand the importance of allowing you to
    express yourself and feel your emotions without trying
    to steer you away from the feelings.

3. **Be unavailable to everyone else.**

    If you're worried about other people interrupting your
    process or being unsupportive of you, tell the neces-
    sary people that you'll be unreachable during that time.
    It's much easier to give yourself space to process when
    other people aren't taking up your extra space. Turn
    your phone off if you need to. Shut your computer
    down. Your space is sacred, so make sure you're pro-
    tecting it.

4. **Plan what to do during the pity party.**

    If you're planning a conscious pity party, chances are that you're already feeling a lot of those negative feelings bubbling up. But if you want to open the gates to those feelings, choose things that tap into them. Pick that one movie or listen to that one album that always brings up your self-pity and sadness. Do things you would normally do when you want to wallow in a breakup. Eat junk food if that feels right to you. Angrily vent or cry to your support person. Journal about the things that have made you a victim. It's important to immerse yourself in the feeling, and ride it out whatever direction it wants to go. Maybe you want to scream at the top of your lungs, or break a plate, or sob for three hours. Let yourself feel what you're feeling. If at any point it feels unsafe, or like it's too much, that's when you call your support to step in.

75

5. **Care for yourself after the party.**

    After a pity party, it's important to use compassionate self-care. Clearing practices are necessary to purify some of the energy that's been released. Taking care of the basics—like sleep, hydration, food, and bathing—will be incredibly important. Spend time talking with your support about the experience, or journaling about it. Give yourself time to adjust before you jump back into normal life. Check in with your feelings, your energy signatures, and see how they feel. If you're having trouble getting out of the difficult feelings that were brought up, turn to your support.

Contraindications: When *Not* to Have a Pity Party

Conscious pity parties are not always for everyone. If you know you're working with some intense trauma, especially in the form of PTSD, it's necessary to have the right support team. There is a difference between making space for your feelings and retraumatizing yourself, and if your triggers are too intense and traumatic, then avoid doing this kind of work by yourself. Always consult with your mental health team and make sure you have the support you need for where you're at in your process.

CHAPTER 5

Whose Feelings ARE These?

I sat on the kitchen floor, my back up against the cabinets. This was my giving-up spot. I wiped away my tears with my sleeve as I clenched my jaw in anger. I'd recently moved in with my partner, and I knew I was supposed to be in the honeymoon phase of cohabitating, but I wasn't. As the weeks went by, I noticed my moods being more unpredictable. I was angry when I didn't have a reason to be angry. I felt listless when I didn't have a reason to be listless. Everything felt a little fuzzy around the edges. Everything was a little unclear. And when he said something that didn't quite sit right with me, I snapped at him. And then my sudden irritation triggered him and he snapped back at me. This continued until I resigned myself to the kitchen floor.

When we both had calmed down, and he joined me on the kitchen floor and finally explained to me how he was feeling, I was alarmed to find that it was the same way I had been feeling. Only, I didn't understand *why* I was feeling it. The more I thought about it, the more it didn't make sense. When I tried to find the root of my anger, I couldn't. My reactions were like echoes of his feelings, but I had no real stake in them. I wasn't *really* angry. I was feeling *him* being angry, and then taking it on as my own. It was like I was becoming him and he was having a fight with himself. It was like I disappeared into his feelings. In that moment of realization, I discovered that I had subconsciously taken on so many of his feelings that I was having trouble figuring out what my own feelings were.

Being an empath means that you can feel other people's emotions, but it also means that you can disappear inside of them. Confusing the energies is a common problem. What are *their* feelings and what are *mine*? The more the empath coexists with others without proper boundaries and ways to discern their own energy, the messier and more confusing things get.

It gets even worse when triggering emotions are involved. It gets easier, though. By working with your energy signatures, your intuition, and what triggers you, you can easily discern which feelings belong to you and which feelings belong to others.

Turn to Your Energy Signatures

Feeling bombarded by the feelings of others is exhausting. It takes a toll. It not only distorts your relationships with other people, but it also distorts your relationship with yourself and your dreams and your goals.

Working with your emotions and creatively describing them so you can recognize their energy signatures will be your greatest strength in discerning whether the energy you feel is yours or someone else's. For example, if you're with your partner and you're feeling some anger that you don't know the source of, you can feel into that energy, and if you recognize the energy signature, that energy is yours.

Maybe you've named your anger emotion Claude, and his energy feels snobby and has an orange haze, and you were able to feel that energy while arguing with your partner. If that's the case, you can hang out with Claude, trace that anger back, and find the source of it. Once you know it's yours, you can hold space for yourself, even asking your partner to hold space for it as well. If you feel into the energy and it's an energy signature you don't recognize, like you're building a new character you've never met before, that energy is probably not yours, and it's time to separate yourself from it. Essentially, you're going to know yourself *so* well that you will know exactly what belongs to you and what doesn't. You may even get to know the energy signatures of your loved ones, which makes it even easier to discern between theirs and yours.

Knowing yourself that well takes time and space. To truly process and identify your own emotions, you need some time away from everyone else. Separating from others gives you the space to let everyone else's energy fall away so you can focus on your own. Sometimes that means you will have to excuse yourself from others so you can process on your own. Sometimes that means pushing the pause button on an argument or temporarily walking away from decision-making. Taking time to examine emotions on your own is an important way to hold space for yourself and your skills as an empath. You'll find more ways to create this space in Energetic Clearing Tools in the resources section.

Using Yes and No Intuition

Tuning into your body is an exercise in listening to your intuition, which can help you discern energies. Your body can give you distinct signals to indicate whether you're on track or not. To tune in, all you have to do is get into a relaxed position and do a few minutes of deep breathing.

When you feel relaxed, you can ask your body, *What is my "yes"*? When your intention is focused on your body, your body will respond to your question by producing specific sensations. Those sensations can differ from person to person. My yes feels like an expansion, like my chest rises and my shoulders straighten, and I feel like I could stretch into as much as space as I'd like. You might feel something similar, or maybe butterflies in your stomach, or tingling in your third eye.

Once you've discovered your yes sensations, you can then ask your body, *What's my "no"*? Your body will respond to the new question and produce completely different sensations. My no feels like my body is contracting and collapsing into itself.

You might experience a sinking feeling, or your shoulders might hunch over.

Knowing your yes and no can help you identify your own feelings and separate yourself from the feelings of others. If you feel overwhelmed with emotions and you're not sure if they're yours or someone else's, ask yourself, *Does this feeling of dread belong to me?*

If that feeling is yours, your body will respond with your yes sensations. If it's not, it will respond with your no sensations.

This works especially well for discerning whether another person is good for you or not. Since empaths are often vulnerable to narcissists and those who would exploit our compassion, having discernment when it comes to others is paramount. If you're getting strong no sensations in your body when you're with a certain person, especially if it's a romantic partner, your intuition is telling you that it's time to walk away. If you feel yes sensations when you're with another person, your body is opening up to love and trust in a positive way.

81

This technique only works if you use it frequently, for both small things and big things. When you feel intense emotions, sometimes those emotions themselves will create physical sensations in your body, which could confuse your yes and no sensations. If you start with small, seemingly meaningless situations to use your yes and no sensations, you'll start to build a trust in your body.

One of my favorite ways to start small is by asking myself questions throughout the day. I'll ask myself, *Does my body want kale salad for lunch today?* or *Do I want to watch trashy reality TV tonight?* or *Should I go out with my friend this weekend?* By starting with decisions that don't seem to carry a lot of weight, you learn your intuitive craft in a way that takes the pressure off and may actually surprise you.

Sometimes I *really* don't want kale salad and sometimes I *really* want to watch trashy TV. And surprisingly, those decisions can end up being healthy decisions. My body may give me no sensations with kale salad one day, because my digestion just needs some cooked food. Or my body may give me yes sensations to trashy TV, because what I really need is some time and space to relax and take my mind off things. I've often intuitively said no to social engagements, even though I wanted to go, and discovered the next day that I was sick and couldn't go anyway. I've also intuitively said yes to social engagements, even though I was feeling depressed, and ended up having an incredibly healing time with friends.

By using this technique frequently in a variety of situations—even the small ones—while also realizing how your emotions affect you, you'll be able to fine-tune your responses and understand yourself and your body on a whole new level. Your body holds an entire universe of knowledge, just waiting to be utilized by you.

82

It should be noted, however, that communicating freely with the body like this isn't always possible. For those with a history of trauma who may have difficulties with disassociation, making the mind/body connection is a little more complicated. This is totally normal and okay.

Another way to use your yes and no intuition, even if you can't sink into your body quite yet, is to assign your yes and your no an intuitive visual signal. Let's say you assign your yes the color purple, and you assign your no the color orange. Start by asking yourself yes or no questions you already know the answer to, and intentionally visualize the color for the right answer. You're creating a visual association to those two colors in your mind, so when it comes time for you to use yes and no intuition, you begin to intuitively see the color purple when it's a yes and the color orange when it's a no.

Working with Your Triggers

Uh-oh…it's happened.

You've been triggered.

You feel an onslaught of frantic painful emotions, defensiveness, and your fight-or-flight response is activated. You're ready to either jump down their throat or shut down completely. What do you do now?

Being triggered is a psychological response to something that reminds you of your trauma. The trigger could be a smell, a certain phrase, a tone of voice, or any stimulus that causes your brain to bring up the memory of your trauma, making you feel like you're reliving it to a certain degree. When you're triggered, your body and mind may react as if they're experiencing the trauma all over again.

As overwhelming as they may feel, your triggers are actually a good thing. (I know, that seems really untrue and annoying, but stay with me.) Your triggers offer you clear insight into the areas where you need healing and awareness. Triggers happen because a wound has been activated, and your natural defenses want to prevent any more pain in that wound. That's why you feel defensive.

Triggers also pull you down into negative neural pathways, into the pathways your trauma created. Your brain is wired with a lot of repetitive, conditioned thinking. The more you think a certain thought, the more that thought carves a pathway. That pathway becomes more worn the more you go back to that thought, and before long, you find it hard to choose another path. This is why your triggers are always related to your past.

The first thing to do when you feel triggered is to stop and make space for it. Your trigger is like a toddler having a temper tantrum, so it's important to stop and pay attention. This could be when you excuse yourself from the fight you're having

83

with your partner so you can be alone to go through it. If you have an understanding partner, you could ask them to allow you to walk yourself through the trigger with them. More often than not, though, I recommend being alone, especially if you're new to confronting your triggers.

When you're in a safe space, name your feeling out loud. Your initial feeling may be completely different from the feeling you end up with after the process, but that first frantic feeling is very important. Speaking that feeling out loud gives it validation, and naturally begins to create more space for it.

Ask yourself, *Why am I feeling that feeling?*

Answer your own question. The answer is probably going to be something your partner did or said.

Ask yourself, *Why did that bother me so much?*

Answer that question, and then ask yourself *Why?* again.

This process will be a series of questions until you boil down your responses as much as you can, getting to the truth behind them. Each answer will peel away more and more of what the other person said or did to you, and each answer will bring you further and further back toward your core wounding, and what happened to you in the past. Once you reach your core wounding, you're able to see that the pain you're feeling isn't just from the person who triggered you. The pain is from years of living with your core wound—years of feeling unseen, or unsupported, or abused. Once you reach this, use the core wound exercises in the Do Your Work section of chapter 3 to work on your healing. You can choose to share this exploration with the person who triggered you or not— that is up to you. But every time you trace your trigger back, you have another opportunity to heal yourself.

Here's an example: Julia sent a text to her husband, Mark, in the middle of a busy day, asking him to stop at the store on his way home to buy milk for the kids. They were completely out. Mark agreed.

When Mark got home, he came in empty-handed. Julia asked him what happened, and he said that he just forgot.

This action completely triggered Julia into anger, and Mark couldn't understand why something as small as a forgotten gallon of milk would upset her so much.

Julia went into her room to have some time alone.

I am really angry, she said to herself.

Why are you angry?

Because Mark forgot to bring home milk, even though he agreed to earlier.

Why does that upset you?

Because he never listens to me. It's like he just ignores me if it doesn't have anything to do with him.

Why does feeling ignored hurt so much?

Because it means that he doesn't care about me or my needs or the needs of his children. He only cares about himself.

Why does it hurt so much to have your needs ignored?

It turned out that Julia had an alcoholic mother as a child. Her mother would forget to provide basic needs, like milk, and would ignore or forget her children's requests. Julia experienced so much neglect, even on the basic level of being fed, that her brain was wired to believe that her needs weren't important.

When Mark—who usually did his best when it came to the needs of his family—forgot the milk because of an oversight, he triggered Julia's core wound of neglect. When Julia was able to realize her trigger, she explained the situation to Mark, who then agreed to be more mindful of the things that could cause her more pain. He was also able to reassure her that her needs were important. Julia was also able to see that she needed to do more work around her self-worth and with

85

her inner child, and was able to meet her anger with love and understanding.

Your triggers always trace back to a wounding, usually some version of your core wound. If you can practice the patience it takes to question yourself until you've traced your trigger all the way back to the root of where it hurts, you can shift the way you communicate entirely. Once you understand that experiencing a trigger means that you are experiencing a past pain that needs love, the trigger immediately loses its charge. You'll also realize that whenever someone else is triggered, they're experiencing that same wounding, which makes you more compassionate with them and less likely to continue arguing. You'll begin to associate "what is triggering" with "what needs love."

Triggers as Mirrors

Tracing your triggers back is one way to see how people are mirrors, reflecting back what's inside of us. One thing to keep in mind, however, is that even though people are mirrors, that doesn't mean it's all about your reflection all the time. Sometimes people will remind you of all the wounding you have inside of yourself and offer a chance to dig into that. Other times, people are simply being jerks, and by focusing on your own reflection every single time, that person will continue being a jerk to you. Let's look at this distortion.

Truth: *We're all mirrors to each other.*

Our relationships are examples of our own projections, perceptions, and experiences. People are often brought into our lives to light up specific issues and boundaries within us— both in loving, positive ways and in tumultuous, harmful ways.

When you don't like how someone reacts to you, it can be indicative of something inside of yourself and not about the other person at all. When someone doesn't like the way you react to them, it can be indicative of something inside of them and not about you at all. Relationships are the greatest teachers in that they reflect so many things back to us. Sometimes our reactions reflect the work we need to do on ourselves and the healing we need.

Also truth: *These mirrors are funhouse mirrors.*

They bend and distort what is really happening. What you may see isn't necessarily true. If someone reacts badly to you, maybe they're just being a jerk and it has nothing to do with what you need to heal or reflect upon. If you brush off someone's feelings about how you're treating them because you just *know* it's about them, maybe you're the jerk and you're bypassing their valid experiences. You can never fully understand the reality of what is happening between two people at any given moment in any given relationship.

Because we're so absorbed in our own reflections within our relationships, we often overlook the *actual* other person and instead assign them an idea relating to ourselves rather than an identity all their own. You simply cannot subscribe to the "we're just mirrors" concept 100 percent without turning into either a smug bypassing jerk who discounts someone else's important life experiences or a disempowered martyr. Balance and discernment make all the difference.

As an empath, since it's already so easy to get energies mixed up, it's especially important to honor the role of triggers while also separating out your experience from the experience of the other person. You are each having an individual experience, even though it's being reflected through one another.

Keeping this in mind as you work with your triggers will help you separate your energy from theirs.

Using Neutrality

When dealing with our difficult emotions and the emotions of others, neutrality is a powerful tool. Contrary to popular belief, in this case, neutrality doesn't mean that you don't have any feelings. Neutrality means that you can allow yourself to have whatever feelings you have but without acting upon them. Neutrality means that you can allow other people to have whatever feelings they have but without reacting to them.

When we experience our triggers at the same time our loved ones experience their triggers, our energies get mixed together really easily. The more upset we are, the harder it is to determine whose feeling is whose.

Taking space and processing your triggers alone when they come up is one way to practice neutrality in relationships. By falling prey to your triggers and reacting to them with anger, you're reaching deep inside yourself, pulling that energy out, and throwing it at the other person. When they react to their triggers, they're doing the same thing to you. Eventually, there's so much intense energy being thrown around that it's no wonder we can't differentiate whose energy is whose!

Taking space to process your triggers alone doesn't mean that you don't get to have your feelings. Your feelings, even the triggered ones, are all valid. By separating yourself from the conflict, though, you create a container for your triggers and your emotions to be understood in a healthy way. Once you know you can create a safe space for your own feelings, you can more easily talk about them with your loved ones.

Knowing how to do this will also help you keep your loved ones' energies from mixing too much with yours, because you

88

will know to avoid reacting when they are clearly triggered. You can allow them to have their trigger and hold your own boundaries at the same time. You know that their trigger isn't a true reflection of the current situation, so you don't have to take it personally. By doing this, you are holding space for them and their emotions. This doesn't mean it's okay for your loved ones to consistently take out their frustration and their triggers on you, but knowing how to handle it will keep your energies from getting confused, while also validating your loved ones' emotions.

Demonstrating a healthy way to handle triggers with your loved ones will make it easier for them to communicate with you too. If they see that what you're doing helps you to understand things and calm down, they will likely want to learn how to do the same thing. Nobody wants to have triggers; they just don't know their other options yet.

Learning your own triggers like the back of your hand will help you discern how to handle your relationships with other people. Using your yes/no body intuition will help you discern which relationships are healthy and which are not. I want you to have all the tools to meet your triggers with love and understanding, because you deserve the lightness that comes from healing yourself.

89

DO THE WORK

Discerning whose feelings are whose is a challenge. The tools in this section will help you hone your discernment skills.

Yes and No Intuition

Sit comfortably. Close your eyes, and spend a few minutes focusing on your breathing: take deep, slow breaths, inhaling through your nose for a count of three (1-2-3), holding for a count of three, and exhaling through your mouth for a count of three. Do this until you feel your body relax.

When you start feeling relaxed, move your awareness from your toes up to your head, saying hello to all of your body. Say hello to your legs, your hips, your chest, your arms. Silently give thanks to your body as you do this. By doing this, you're letting your body know that you love it and want to communicate with it.

When you're ready, take another deep breath. Ask your body, *What is my yes sensation?* And then focus on steady breathing as you wait to feel your yes sensation. It might be a tingle in your third eye, or the feeling of heat in your belly, or the feeling of your chest expanding outward. Let that feeling grow strong enough to where you know you'll be able to recognize it later.

When you feel clear on what your yes is, ask your body, *What is my no sensation?* Again, focus on steady breathing as you wait for your no sensation. It might be the feeling of your shoulders contracting or a poke in your ankle.

90

Even though you are communicating with your body for this exercise, your sensation may not be strictly physical. It may be an energetic feeling. You may experience your chest expanding for your yes sensation, but your physical chest may not actually expand. Depending on how you experience your intuition, your sensation could be completely physical or largely intuitive.

If connecting to your body is a struggle because of past trauma and dissociation, you can use color visualization instead. Assign a specific color for your yes and a specific color for your no before you begin asking questions. With intention and focus, begin asking yourself yes or no questions you already know the answers to. When you ask yourself a question with the answer of yes, visualize the color you've chosen for your yes. When you ask yourself a question with the answer of no, visualize the color you've chosen for your no. Once you've trained your brain and your intuition to use those colors, you can start asking questions you don't know the answer to; observe which of the two colors you see in your mind.

Trace Back Your Triggers

Your first step in tracing back your trigger is to step away from the situation that's triggered you. If you're arguing with a significant other, tell them you need a moment to yourself and go to another room. If it's a situation at work, excuse yourself to use the bathroom. Do whatever you can to give yourself the physical space you need to look at your trigger before you react out of anger. If you're with someone who understands the work you're doing, you can tell them that you're feeling triggered and that you need them to hold space for you while you work it out. Most often, though, you'll want to process it alone.

Once you've stepped away from the situation, the first thing to do is name your feeling out loud. Even if you know that's not the feeling you'll end up with, even if you know you're overreacting, you have to be able to name out loud that first frantic feeling after you've been triggered. By naming it out loud, you create space for the feeling to express itself.

91

After naming that feeling out loud, answer these questions:

Why do I feel this way?
(The answer will most likely be a statement that
blames the other person for what they said or did,
and that is totally okay and necessary.)

↓

Why did what the other person did or said bother me so much?

↓

Why is it important for me to not feel that way?

Continue asking yourself these "why" questions with the intention that each answer will peel away more and more of what the other person said or did to you, and each answer will bring you further and further back toward your core wounding, and what happened to you in the past.

Once you reach your core wound, you're able to see that the pain you're feeling isn't just from the person who triggered you. The pain is from years of living with your core wound—years of feeling unseen, or unsupported, or abused. Now use the exercises on core wounds in the Do Your Work section of chapter 3 to work on your healing. Remember that every time you trace your trigger back, you have another opportunity to heal yourself.

CHAPTER 6

Working
with
Boundaries

Boundaries, boundaries, boundaries—one of the biggest topics for empath gripe sessions.

"You need to set your boundaries!"

"You have no boundaries!"

"OMG, they totally ignored your boundaries!"

Don't get me wrong. Boundaries really are the bread and butter of healthy empathy. Boundaries are the rules we set for our own existence. The quality of our lives is completely dependent on our boundaries, since they are the gatekeepers of whether we accept, reject, or alter a situation.

But they're actually a lot easier than you think. Knowing your boundaries and enforcing them will become easier the more connected you are to yourself. Respecting your own boundaries is almost like a practice in muscle memory. Once you teach yourself the habit, it becomes more and more automatic. Soon enough, respecting your boundaries will be as automatic as brushing your teeth before bed or walking your dog each morning.

94

The Secret to Working with Boundaries

I'm going to let you in on a little secret that will completely change the way you look at your boundaries. You know how we're always saying that we need to build better boundaries? Well…you don't have to build anything.

Let me repeat that: you don't have to build anything. There is nothing to build.

The truth about boundaries is that they already exist in their perfect form for every single situation. Your boundaries are actually already in place all the time. It's not your job to build your boundaries; it's your job to be aware of where they already are.

Think of yourself as operating from two different levels at the same time. First and foremost, you're operating as your higher self. Your higher self knows exactly what's up, and they're wise as hell, so they've already figured out your needs and your boundaries. They work with your energy body to move and adjust your boundaries accordingly for every situation and relationship you find yourself in. It's natural for them to do this, since your higher self works in the spirit world, and they do it with grace and ease.

The other level you operate from is your human self. Your human self abides by physical human laws like time and physics, so they're a little behind your higher self. They get bogged down by heavy energy, and because they operate from that physical body, the process of clearing and integrating energy is a slower and denser ordeal. Your human self is always playing catch-up with your spirit.

Your only job, when it comes to building your boundaries, is to establish a truer connection to your higher self and to establish an awareness of the boundaries that already exist.

95

You know when someone disrespects your boundaries, even though you had no idea it was a boundary for you yet? You know that sinking feeling you get? That's because on some level, you already knew your boundaries, so that feeling of someone crossing them feels like an internal betrayal, like a ping of sadness coming from the disconnect between you and your higher self.

Once you've developed a dialogue between your human self and your higher self, you will always know where your boundaries are. If you're struggling with your boundaries, you can ask your higher self where the edges of those boundaries are. Your higher self is the gatekeeper and always knows your edges. You'll be able to see the moments when you betray yourself by ignoring your boundaries, and you'll be able to see the moments when you are betrayed by others ignoring them. In the Do the Work section, you'll find an exercise on getting to know your gatekeeper.

Know the Spectrum

Your boundaries manifest themselves on a spectrum, and knowing where you fall on it will help you find the right balance for yourself.

One end of the spectrum is the "not enough" side. This is where your boundaries have been underutilized and where you haven't discovered your edges yet. Being on this end will make you extra vulnerable to other people's energies. This will cause uncontrollable weepiness, powerlessness, and hyper-fragility. This is the end where everyone crosses your boundaries all the time, leaving you exhausted and overwhelmed.

On the other end of the spectrum is the "too much" side. This happens when you've attempted to create firm boundaries for yourself, and by trying to protect yourself, you've built solid steel walls instead of flexible boundaries. Being on this end keeps the bad out, but it also keeps the good out. This end will keep you invulnerable to others, but it also leaves you lonely. You may find yourself out of touch with your own sense of compassion and empathy, and you may find that no one can truly reach you.

Where do you find yourself on that spectrum? Most empaths have found themselves on either end at different times as they've tried to deal with the realities of being so sensitive, but one side usually predominates.

How have you been too soft and yielding?

How have you been too rigid and cold?

Can you think of a few instances in your life where you felt like your boundaries were constantly being betrayed, or where

96

you felt like you couldn't let the good in because you were so preoccupied with keeping out the bad? I want you to find a balance in the middle. I want you to have a strong but flexible identity in your own boundaries—strong enough to keep you in your own power, but not so strong that you keep yourself locked away behind a wall.

You can also use these feelings to create specific energy signatures. You can create an energetic signature for boundaries that are too yielding, and an energetic signature for boundaries that are too rigid. This will assist you in knowing when you're swinging too far one way or the other.

Even though boundaries can be a really complicated subject, simplifying them makes everything easier. Knowing that your higher self already has your boundaries perfectly constructed for you will take the pressure off building them. You only need to tune in and feel where they are.

97

Ground Yourself

How can you tune into those preexisting boundaries? The first step is always to ground yourself. *Grounding* is an important process that keeps your energy stable. The general concept is that when grounding, you connect into the energy of the earth and draw excess energy in your body to your feet to be stabilized in the ground.

That excess energy is usually found in your higher chakras and, if not grounded, can lead to anxiety and spiritual madness. Many spiritual types exist primarily in their higher chakras, and they often become out of touch with reality because all of that energy, even if it's generally a good energy, isn't stabilized.

Because your boundaries are there to protect your physical body *and* your spiritual body, grounding both your physical and spiritual energy is necessary. And because your physical body is slower to integrate energy, it's especially important to be connected to your body and take steps to ensure it's being taken care of.

Grounding can be as simple as a visualization of connecting with the earth, sticking your toes in the sand at the beach, walking in the woods barefoot, or doing something physical that's enjoyable.

When you ground, your spiritual energy is distributed evenly throughout your body and your chakras. That kind of balance is key to becoming more aware of your boundaries, and will make your ability to see and enforce them all the more powerful.

What are some of the ways that you already intuitively ground yourself? Do you like to hike? Do you love the feeling of burying your feet in the sand? Do you notice yourself being drawn to the color red in times when you need grounding? Red is the color of the root chakra and is the best color for quick assistance with grounding. Maybe you already tend to eat a lot of root vegetables or warm foods or chocolate when you need grounding.

Build a practice of grounding out of things you already love to do. Make grounding a part of your everyday ritual. Be intentional with the foods you eat and the way you move your body. In the Do the Work section at the end of this chapter, you'll find a grounding visualization that can be done easily every day.

Feel Your Edges

Once you've grounded your energy, you're in a better place to be able to feel where your boundaries are. You can then use your yes/no body intuition and your energy signatures to help determine the details. Remember the sensations you felt with your yes and your no? Remember the energy signatures you built? Those sensations are related to your boundaries, and you can test them out in any situation.

If you're wondering where your boundaries are with your coworkers, imagine various scenarios and situations where they're involved, and with each imagined scenario, notice your sensations. If one situation gives you strong no sensations, then you've found the edges of your boundaries where you need to turn back. If another situation gives you strong yes sensations, then your boundaries are already healthy and active. To take it a step further, after you've imagined a scenario with strong no sensations, you can then imagine how you would change the situation to feel like a yes. Simply following your feelings and your body cues will help you find the edges and the curves of all your boundaries. This is an exercise in imagination, and all the creative work you've done with your victim, your villain, and your energy signatures will make this process easier.

This process is even clearer when you work with it in person. There's some trial and error involved, but it's completely worth the effort. Start feeling out your yes and no sensations and energy signatures when you're working through your relationships. Notice the sensations when you answer questions in certain ways or when you're spoken to in a certain manner. Does it feel like a betrayal or an expansion? Does it feel like a yes or a no? Does it feel like a certain energy signature you've built?

One thing I want you to be especially aware of when you work with your boundaries is how you feel when you agree to do something out of obligation or guilt. Since empaths are natural caretakers, you might be agreeing to things beyond your capabilities because you want to be helpful in your

99

relationships. Your body may give you a very specific sensation that lets you know you're crossing your own boundaries.

As you become more aware of your yes and no sensations, you'll feel your no sensations of contraction and shrinking when you agree to do things past your energy level. Eventually, you'll get stronger and adjust to saying no to things when you're feeling the no sensations. Even if you're worried about how people will react, the satisfaction and power you'll feel when you respect your boundaries will far outweigh any temporary guilt.

Know Your Reserves

When working with your boundaries, it's important for you to know your energy reserves and what typically drains or energizes you. If you know your own history and habits, you'll have a clearer path to empowered boundaries.

Take stock of the people who drain you, the places that drain you, the tasks that drain you. All those things that suck the joy right from your life are areas where your boundaries are needed. If you have a people-pleasing habit, you'll find yourself giving away to others the energy you need for yourself. If you have a habit of making yourself smaller for romantic relationships, you can prepare yourself for future relationships by being aware of it. Knowing your weak spots is half the battle, and this is why we've spent so much time identifying and personifying your negative feelings.

Oftentimes, becoming aware is not enough, and we have to let go of some of the people and things that drain us. Consistently taking stock of your life and the people in it will help you realize what needs to be released.

Take stock of the people who bring you joy and energize you, the places and jobs that energize you. You need more of

100

these types of people and places. This is what you need to make more space for. Feeling in flow and in joy is like an automatic exercise in strengthening your boundaries. It's positive reinforcement for your spirit. As you let go of the draining things, you're also making more room for the energizing things to enter into your life.

Knowing your energy reserves at all times will help you realize what you need more of and what you need less of to balance that energy. If you know you've spent much more time on the draining things than the energizing things recently, you'll know it's time to step away from some of the draining things. You'll know it's time to step into some more joy. If you've spent a lot of time in joy recently and feel energized, you may happily agree to do a few extra tasks to help someone out. Your decisions and answers to others will change frequently depending on your energy reserves. Being in tune with them will help you engage with the edges of your boundaries in every situation.

Give Yourself Permission

I know how much you've given to your loved ones. I know how much you've offered and sacrificed. You've ignored your own boundaries for so long that you may not even know what they are right now. And that's okay. I know you've always ignored your boundaries with good intentions. You've always wanted to be a source of good for others. It's a commendable act, but aren't you tired? Aren't you completely and simultaneously exhausted and overwhelmed?

It's time to give yourself permission to stop. I know it feels like the world will stop if you stop, but I promise you, it won't. Give yourself permission to let go of those things that drain you, to say no.

Give yourself permission to rest. Give yourself permission to disappoint others and to choose yourself over them. Give yourself permission to lose the relationships that aren't good for you. Give yourself permission to be powerful.

I know it seems like having an exhausted sort of love is better than no love at all, but the love you'll find when you give yourself permission to just *be yourself* is stronger than any half-love you've ever experienced. It's worth it to lose the ones who won't respect your boundaries. You deserve to make space for those who want to come into your life, fully supportive of you, respectful of your boundaries. Those people will love you *more* because of your boundaries, not less.

Give yourself permission.

Speak Your Truth

102 This is a hard one, I know. Speaking your truth takes practice, because it naturally comes along with some rejection. When it comes to your boundaries though, it's an absolute must. You must be able to verbalize your boundaries.

Let me repeat that one: you must be able to verbalize your boundaries.

Even if you have done all the work to figure out where your boundaries are, it won't do you any good if you can't verbalize them. I wish I could say that people are all naturally intuitive and can pick up on your boundaries without you telling them, but that's simply not the case. Humans have an inherent love of blindness, so they will not see your boundaries. Even with our closest loved ones, we cannot assume that they will naturally pick up on our boundaries. We have to tell them. If we cannot tell them our boundaries, how can we expect them to know and respect them?

All of this difficult emotional work you've done here also essentially creates a guidebook for others to understand you better. If you love yourself and understand yourself, you will be able to tell your loved ones how to love and understand you too. Knowing and communicating your boundaries will strengthen the relationships with the capacity for growth. The clearer you can be about yourself and what you need, the less room you leave for messy situations and misunderstandings, which will make your relationships easier.

This goes both ways too. If you're unclear about someone else's boundaries, ask. Know that for you to understand your loved ones better, you need to know their boundaries too.

When They Don't Respect Your Boundaries

Change is hard. It's not just hard for you. It's hard for everyone in your life.

103

When you begin to assert your boundaries and show signs of change and growth, it may activate some hostility in your loved ones, especially in family members and close friends. They may be angry with you. They have become accustomed to the way you are, and it may feel unsafe for them when you consciously choose not to engage in the same patterns anymore.

If you set new rules for the relationship with your boundaries, and you no longer participate in the same patterns with them, then they can no longer participate in them with you. This is a scary thing for a lot of people. When your changing involves them changing on some level, they could reject it entirely, especially if they have no interest in changing.

On a basic level, when you change, your loved ones fear losing you. It's a legitimate fear, because when you emotionally transform, the old you indeed dies. When you set new rules with your boundaries, you no longer hold the space for the you who settled for the old rules. When you change the rules, your loved ones have to grieve the death of the old you that existed in the old rules. *You* have to grieve the death of the old you. In some cases, becoming more in tune with your intuition and your boundaries means you will have to let some people go. The people who can't or won't adjust to and respect your boundaries are not meant to be close to you anymore, and that's a tough pill to swallow, especially when you love those people.

Your relationships naturally transform as a by-product of you transforming. The ones that respect your boundaries and are capable of growth will bloom in new and beautiful ways, and the ones that don't respect your boundaries and aren't willing to grow will shrivel up and die. It's a harsh reality, but it's a reality. You may find yourself trying to keep certain relationships alive, and despite all the effort, they simply don't align with you anymore.

Being able to let go of what's dead is difficult, but it's a sign of great wisdom and acceptance. Knowing that your new life with your new rules will be even better than all the ones before it will be the balm that soothes the pain.

Voluntary Energetic Blindness

Being an empath means feeling everything all the time. It's exhausting. It's also distracting. Feeling everyone's feelings can take away the time and energy you need for yourself. If we're using our energy reserves on other people's feelings that aren't relevant to us, we're losing our power. No wonder we

104

can feel so powerless and overwhelmed. We have no energy left for our own damn problems!

There's a way to fix this. We can use voluntary energetic blindness to cope with some of the extra energy we simply don't want to feel.

Voluntary energetic blindness is like a setting you can turn on with your higher self. You can tell your higher self that you simply don't have the time or energy to deal with other people's crap, so you choose to not let it in. This is a survival tool, one you can use to whatever extent you need it. At the end of this chapter, there is a helpful visualization to activate this setting.

Remember: everything is a negotiation—especially with your higher self and with the Universe. If something isn't working out for you, you can negotiate different terms with your higher self. If the way you experience energy causes trouble for you, you can tell the Universe the ways you'd prefer to experience it. The Universe is actually fairly accommodating to those who speak bravely out loud. (This is a great exercise in verbalizing your boundaries!)

Speak to your higher self. Tell them you want to turn on your voluntary energetic blindness to the excess energy you don't want to deal with right now. And as situations arise where you feel someone else reaching out for your energy in a way that doesn't feel empowering to you, choose to use that voluntary blindness and walk away.

DO THE WORK

Knowing that you don't have to create your own boundaries is a relief. You still need to learn, however, where your boundaries are. These exercises will help.

Get to Know Your Gatekeeper

Your gatekeeper is a version of your higher self whose only job is to take care of your boundaries. Your gatekeeper adjusts your boundaries perfectly for every situation in every relationship and encounter. *Your* job is to communicate with your gatekeeper so they can let you know where your boundaries lie.

To do this, close your eyes and visualize your gatekeeper. What do they look like? What are they wearing? What does the gate look like that they're protecting? What's their name? Notice how they speak to you. They're an all-knowing authority on your boundaries, so they may be quite forceful in their communication. Gatekeepers usually have a pretty interesting sense of humor too, so take your time in getting to know them. Ask them their preferred method of communicating. Maybe they'll have a certain bodily signal, or a phrase or sensation they'll use when they communicate with you. Put all of these details in your journal, and make sure to check in with your gatekeeper on a regular basis. Your gatekeeper will have different moods for different situations, so it's important to get to know their patterns and moods and how they relate to what's happening in your life. The more you work with them, the more it will become an easy line of communication for you to reference every day.

106

Grounding Visualization

Close your eyes and spend a few minutes on deep breathing. Visualize a bright red tube of light coming up from the center of the earth. This red light, this pure earth energy, is going to be absorbed through your feet. See the red light being absorbed into your body, up your legs, and slowly rising up through your chakras. Then visualize a white tube of light coming down from the heavens. This is pure divine energy, and it's being absorbed into your body through your crown chakra. See this energy being absorbed, moving slowly down through your chakras.

You are completely connected to the earth, and completely connected to the heavens. Notice that at your heart chakra, the red light and the white light mix, creating a beautiful soft pink right over your heart. This energy is unconditional love, and it feels soft and safe. In this moment, you are connected to everything, and your heart is the meeting point of heaven and earth.

Boundaries Checklist

When figuring out how to use your boundaries, it can be helpful to use this checklist to see where you're getting stuck.

- ☐ Are you grounded? If not, engage in a grounding activity, or use the grounding visualization above.

- ☐ Can you feel your edges? Are you sensing where your energy gets prickly, or where your accommodation for others stops? If not, use your energy signatures and yes/no body intuition to find out where your edges are.

- ☐ Do you know your energy reserves? Do you know how much energy you have to give? If not, take stock of your recent experiences and how energized or drained you are.

- ☐ Are you giving yourself permission? Do you know where you boundaries are, but you're afraid to use them because of how someone might react? Do you feel secretly ashamed of needing what you need? If you're stuck in the shame or guilt, use your energy signature of those feelings and spend some time on the sacred expression of those feelings.

- ☐ Have you verbalized your boundaries out loud? If you haven't spoken your truth, you can't expect others to respect it. If you're having trouble speaking your truth, revisit the item above and figure out which feelings prevent you from speaking.

107

Voluntary Energetic Blindness Visualization

Relax and close your eyes. Spend a few minutes on deep breathing. Visualize yourself outside of a beautiful temple. A porch, which can be any style you want, wraps around the entire temple. The porch might be made of stone or of wood. This wraparound porch represents your boundaries, and it protects your temple, which represents your pure spirit. Visualize yourself walking slowly on this wraparound porch.

It's a leisurely stroll, but you're also doing a security check. There are steps from the ground up onto the porch, and these are the places where others can reach you. As you walk, visualize large pillars of stone on the porch. These pillars are being placed here to protect you from seeing the energies that aren't relevant to you. With these large pillars, you cannot see that excess energy, and that excess energy cannot reach you.

You can always come back and rearrange the pillars based on what you're experiencing, but know that you can place them there for your protection at any time.

CHAPTER 7

Energetic Patterns in Relationships

I once went to the bank to make some changes on my accounts. I sat with a very friendly banker who was eager to help me. He was very chatty and seemed slightly nervous and distracted. As he told me the required documents I would need to make the desired changes, I found myself very confused. I hadn't even heard of the documents he requested, and I knew very well what I actually needed to make the changes. When I questioned him, he reassured me that what he was saying was correct, and I found myself acting as though I suddenly had no idea what I needed for my account. My voice rose in pitch to sound more feminine and helpless, and I said things like "Oh, I had no idea!" and "Wow, that's good to know!" and I didn't argue when he said, "Good thing I was here to tell you these things!"

After I got home, I did some research and found out that the information he had given me was outdated and dead wrong. I had been right all along, and I felt really gross about it. I mentally replayed what had happened and realized I had completely changed my personality and my convictions. I sensed in him a need to be right and automatically responded to it. And without even thinking about it, I made myself smaller to accommodate his unspoken emotional needs.

A week later, I went to a different branch of the bank and saw a woman I'd worked with before. I brought in the proper documents and just said, "Here ya go." She made the changes without a fuss and without expecting any sort of response from me. It was beautiful. I realized then why I'd always subconsciously accepted jobs with women bosses, and why I turned down (or quit after a short period) jobs with male bosses. My empath nature had been culturally attuned to men, especially in authoritative roles, and that kind of automatic response was very unsettling. (Not to mention, it killed my productivity and creativity.) I remember thinking, *If I'm changing myself this much to make a complete stranger feel better, how much am I changing for the people in my life I actually know and love?*

Because empaths are naturally emotionally supportive and regularly fall into the caretaker role, it's easy for the dynamics in relationships to get confusing or unbalanced. There are common emotional and energetic patterns experienced by most empaths, like the pattern of changing yourself to meet the emotional needs of others, even strangers. Knowing these common patterns can help you understand your own relationships and boundaries within those relationships. You'll also be able to take an inventory of your own relationship patterns when you complete the Do the Work section at the end of this chapter.

The Accommodation Chameleon   111

Empaths have an uncanny ability to be able to shift and change themselves to adjust to the person they are with. Being able to feel the feelings of others can be incredibly illuminating, as you can often tap into the unspoken emotional needs of others. The problem with this skill is that in addition to feeling and knowing, empaths also have the inherent need to fulfill and address those unspoken emotional needs. This means that you've probably found yourself acting differently or doing things differently to meet the unspoken needs of the person you're with.

While this automatic longing to fulfill the needs of others comes from a genuinely good place in your heart, you may also find yourself disappearing because of your ability to be an emotional chameleon. You may find yourself acting small to appease others, because you can feel it would make it more comfortable for them. If you do this long enough, you soon realize that you're not even sure who you really are anymore. Or worse, you realize you're betraying yourself by acting small.

Empaths often automatically change their behaviors for others when the other person's emotions are clearly being felt. The empath's emotional needs are then put on the back burner as they tend to the needs of others. While it's an incredible skill to be able to tune into the needs of others around us, we need to be able to realize when and how we're giving away our power in the name of empathy.

It's not your job to meet everyone's emotional needs. It's impossible, and that kind of accommodating nature is as disempowering for the other person as it is for you. Standing tall in your own convictions to meet your own needs, despite the fact that you know you're going against what someone else needs, will empower you in a way that leads to more balance overall.

112

The Distortion of Unconditional Love

Many people strive for unconditional love within their relationships. They use it as a means to forgive others and stand by their people. But is striving for unconditional love always a good thing?

Unconditional love may not be very practical or honest when it comes to the reality of relationships, especially as an empath. Unconditional love, by definition, is love that's not subject to any conditions. The problem with this is that boundaries are conditions. Boundaries are conditions to a healthy relationship, set by each person in the relationship. Boundaries make clear what the person is willing or not willing to accept.

Having unconditional love in practice within your relationship would mean a relationship with no boundaries. No boundaries might seem like a romantic idea for the most advanced of spiritualists, but as long as we remain human on this earth, we require healthy boundaries. The practice of unconditional love could cover up and excuse bad behaviors that continually repeat themselves. For an empath, it's already a challenge to find emotional boundaries with others, and perpetuating the idea that there *shouldn't be* boundaries in love will make it even more difficult to find emotional independence.

What if instead of striving for unconditional love, we strive for healthy boundaries that allow the relationship to grow, evolve, and flourish to the highest good of both partners? If something is no longer for the highest good of each person and it can't be changed to be for the highest good, then it is no longer a healthy relationship.

This doesn't mean you can't have unconditional love for a person. It means that in order to practice unconditional love, you often need to let them go. If that person treats you badly, you can still love them, but you may need to love them from afar, ending that negative behavior. Unconditional love is not a replacement for self-love.

Healthy boundaries are *way* sexier than unconditional love, since they empower both parties in an active, working relationship.

113

The Challenge of Codependency: External vs. Internal Validation

Codependency is a hot topic when it comes to identifying negative patterns in relationships. Unfortunately, codependency is common in the relationships of empaths.

Because empaths are so accustomed to living their lives based on the emotions of others, they can develop low self-esteem. Since we feel so intensely, it's easy to base our lives on external validation—that is, on the feelings and reactions of our loved ones—rather than on internal validation. And the more we base our self-esteem and our worth on external sources, the more we rely on those sources to keep us happy and confident. We often find ourselves in these closed feedback loops with our loved ones, cycling through the same arguments and the same solutions time and time again, without really getting anywhere new.

The only thing we accomplish by doing this is creating a stronger force of codependency, where we cycle through the loop faster and faster, seeking that source of validation we found before. The energy of desperation comes in at this point, making it feel like the affection we receive from the other person is the only thing sustaining us.

When we rely on others for our emotional well-being, it puts way too much pressure on our relationships. If it's a good relationship, it will undoubtedly crumble from the pressure. If it's an abusive relationship, it will perpetuate the negative cycle of abuse, strengthening both the victim mentality *and* the abuser mentality.

Breaking codependency is difficult, but not impossible. Knowing yourself inside and out, and being able to meet your own needs yourself, is the key to having high self-esteem that comes from within. All of the exercises I've had you do in this book are to strengthen your awareness and connection to yourself, and that's what you need for easier relationships. When you know and love your own darkness that well, there will be absolutely no room for the energy of codependence.

Abusive Relationships and Gaslighting

It's all too easy for an empath to slip into an abusive relationship. If we're not connected to our own emotions, and if we confuse our own energy with someone else's, we leave space for others to slip in and decide for us what our feelings are.

Gaslighting is a manipulation tactic often used by narcissists and sociopaths to plant seeds of doubt in the victim, making them question their own sanity. It's alarmingly easy to succumb to gaslighting if you're already confused and overwhelmed by out-of-control empathy. I'm sure you can relate to this, since when we're going through this self-growth process or even beforehand, we often think, *Am I crazy?* If you're already questioning your sanity, an abuser can confirm that fear and mold your beliefs to benefit them. Not only will that create a codependent dynamic, but it also builds a structure of abuse (built by the abuser) that will seem completely okay to you while you're still in it. The abuser will twist your negative feelings back toward you, making you believe it's all because of something you're doing.

This partially explains why people stay in abusive relationships. If the abuser builds the relationship in a way that explains away all of the victim's negative experiences of the relationship, the victim is left to believe either that it's somehow their fault or that nothing is actually wrong. This will seem normal to them. When the abuser tells them things like "No one will ever love you like I do," or "You're lucky you have me to help you make sense of all your feelings," or "You can never leave me," they will believe it, because they doubt their own sanity. Red flags don't look like red flags while immersed in the relationship.

Breaking away from abusive relationships isn't easy. It can be dangerous too. You may find yourself deprogramming yourself for many years after an abusive relationship that involved gaslighting. This is why physical space is one of the most treasured tools for discovering which energy is yours and which is someone else's when it comes to your relationships. A healthy dose of space is the precursor to all true emotional awareness and realization. Once you've built up your own energy signatures and can identify what is yours and what isn't, you naturally build defenses against abusive types that might seek to gaslight you.

The Lure of the Narcissist

In terms of romantic relationships, the narcissist has a real appeal. It might sound strange, but you can often feel the lure of the narcissist. It's actually fairly common, and there's no shame in being drawn to people like that. There's a simple energetic reason for being so attracted to narcissists.

As an empath, you are constantly bombarded with the energies of others. For the narcissist, their skill is in disguising their true emotional intentions. They've developed a way to cloak their energy in order to avoid being figured out. As an empath, doesn't that sound like a freaking vacation? Being with someone who doesn't immediately overwhelm you with their energy? Being with someone you can't read right away? We often lose our sense of mystery when we can read energy as much as we do, so finding someone cloaked in mystery is pretty damn appealing.

Eventually, the narcissist reveals themselves to be just as overwhelming as everyone else, but at that point, they've conditioned you to be drawn in by the mystery. They've positioned you to be gaslighted.

Being aware of this energetic blind spot will prevent a lot of heartache. Take caution with those who are incredibly

116

difficult to read, and take your time in making any moves with them.

The Empathy and Narcissism Connection

What if I told you that empaths and narcissists were essentially the same kind of people, only with different coping methods for their empathy?

In a world where it's easy for empaths to demonize narcissists, we can lose a certain sense of accountability. It's easy to pin the blame on them without having to examine ourselves. But what if dangerous narcissism was just one extreme on the spectrum of empathy?

I believe that the spectrum of empathy goes from overwhelmed empath, who is trapped doing everything for others, to cold narcissist, who uses their knowledge of others to get what they want. Sensitive beings have to find a way to cope with their empathy. For some, that means they become overwhelmed empaths who feel everything from everyone. For others, that means they slide into a complete lack of empathy—turning it off, essentially. Generally speaking, this is why more narcissists are males, while more self-identified empaths are females.

Female empaths usually find themselves drowning in the emotions of others, because that's part of what their female conditioning taught them; male empaths, on the other hand, usually turn it off completely, because their male conditioning taught them to not experience or express emotions. Both of these empaths still have the ability to feel other people, but each has a different way of coping. The female gives up her power, while the male goes after more and more power. These, of course, are generalizations, and it isn't to say that there aren't female narcissists or male empaths, or that you need to

117

identify as one gender at all to be either. But the energy of years and years of cultural conditioning in gendered roles still runs through us, and by being aware of how these gendered roles operate, it can help us shift the energy. Being able to explore the energy of your prescribed gender role will also help you explore how you experience your own narcissism and empathy.

As an empath, you have the ability to go either way. You may find yourself powerless to resist the emotions of everyone else, and you may also find yourself cold and reveling in your ability to manipulate others. The two are not mutually exclusive, and they are often connected to the state of your boundaries. The more rigid and extreme your boundaries are, the more you will find yourself swinging toward narcissism. The more you deny your boundaries in the first place, the more you will find yourself powerless and overwhelmed.

118

Emotional Labor and the Womb Space

In addition to female empaths being naturally conditioned toward powerlessness, they are also naturally conditioned to do emotional labor for those around them. *Emotional labor* is the work put in to hold space for and process the emotions of others. It's also the tasks given to females that take up a lot of emotional space. This might mean that you're expected to remember all of your husband's family's birthdays, even though he doesn't. This might mean that you're expected to handle the kids when they're crying, while he gets to escape to the bedroom. This might mean that you're expected to plan the parties at work or you're expected to hold space while the men in your life process all their feelings to you.

Take stock of all the emotional labor you do for other people. Since you're an empath, it's all too easy to see what everyone else needs. So naturally, you'd be able to meet those needs, right? How much of your energy is spent processing the emotions of other people? You may be surprised to find how much vitality you lose by agreeing to do more and more emotional labor.

This doesn't mean all emotional labor is bad, though. The largest part of my job is helping others process their emotions, and it's an amazing job. But I'm also getting paid for it. My emotional labor is appreciated and compensated. When it comes to my personal relationships, I allow for a generous amount of emotional labor when it doesn't diminish my energy reserves too much.

What kind of emotional labor do you put in for your family, your partner, your coworkers, your friends? How often are you giving this labor? Is any of your extra emotional labor paid? Know the amount of emotional labor you're putting in, and be aware of how it affects your energy reserves. Adjust accordingly. Saying no in the face of excessive emotional labor will shift your power. No is a sacred word. Use it.

119

One of the main reasons men look to women for their emotional processing is because women have a built-in womb space. The womb space literally creates and houses life. It is a safe space kept only for nourishment. This is where you can turn when you need to mother yourself and take care of yourself. Your womb space holds an incredible amount of safe and comforting energy. Because men don't have that built-in womb space, and because they've been conditioned to avoid their own emotions, they're naturally drawn to your womb space. Their emotions need to go somewhere to be safe, and they can feel that their emotions would be safest with you. This doesn't mean, however, that the male empath can't draw upon his own womb energy for comfort. While having a biological womb space can make it easier, the womb space is as much energetic as it is physical, and focus and intention on that energetic mothering energy is just as effective.

With gender becoming less and less rigid, these energetic roles will naturally begin to shift, and there won't be such a divide. As I said, you don't need a biological womb space to be able to mother yourself nor do you need to be a male to demand emotional labor from others.

We're in the process of creating healthy energetic routines for everyone, regardless of gender. But the acceptance of gender fluidity is still new, and the previous gender roles have been locked in for a very long time, so it will take a lot of awareness to monitor and shift the levels of emotional labor still expected of women.

Your Victim and Your Villain in Your Relationships

It's easy to fall into helplessness when it comes to relationships. With all the difficult things an empath experiences on a daily basis, relationships can often feel like the heaviest burden instead of the joy we wish them to be.

When an empath becomes overwhelmed or scared in the face of a relationship, their shadow usually comes out. It's easier to let your victim or your villain take the reins in your relationships rather than to stay present with the fear. Your victim will want to take control, blaming everything on the other person and believing everything is a move against them. Your villain will take the vengeful route, trying to protect themselves from becoming the victim, and will intentionally do things to gain the upper hand in the relationship. Your victim wants to give up their power. Your villain wants to gain all of the power.

If your parents have triggered you, your victim may step in and blame your entire life on their poor decisions. If your lover has triggered you, your villain may step in to intentionally manipulate them. Both victim and villain try to prevent you from feeling the full pain of the trigger.

Jade found herself drawn to dark, intense, dramatic relationships. She enjoyed the game of it, the play of predator and prey. They all started with fireworks and unrivaled passion, and they all blew up in betrayal and smoke. Her lovers ended up as her mortal enemies. I had her personify her inner villain for me.

Her inner villain was a dark sex kitten, a woman who deeply hated men and wanted to guiltlessly consume them like a siren bringing down ships at sea. As she described her villain and her relationships, we realized she was letting her villain completely control her relationships. Jade had *become* her inner villain when it came to her romantic relationships. She loved, and she wanted to be loved, but her desire to destroy and consume was driving her relationships.

121

There was no possible way she could experience a healthy relationship if she continued to allow her villain to take the reins. Even though her villain was ultimately trying to protect her, she knew that she had to reclaim her power over her relationships, putting her villain in the backseat.

Amber was in the midst of a separation from her husband. They had both been unfaithful, but she could not shake the betrayal she felt from his infidelity. It consistently overwhelmed her and filled her with rage. She was unable to move on and focus on herself, because she felt so victimized by everything that happened.

Her inner victim was in control, replaying cycles of helplessness and betrayal that completely prevented her from moving toward her new life. It wasn't until Amber spent some time with her inner victim and validated her experiences as a victim that she was able to move into self-responsibility for her own part in the relationship and move forward in her own life.

How have your victim and villain manifested in your relationships? Where do you see each of them coming out? You'll find that when you're feeling triggered, and it's too painful to be present with the trigger and trace it back, your victim or villain will step in and take over.

By seeing where your victim and villain manifest in your relationships, you'll be able to see where you can direct your love and your self-work. You'll be able to feel where you want them to step in and choose to remain present in your trigger instead. Claiming responsibility is one of the hardest tasks for an overwhelmed empath, but claiming responsibility is the same as claiming power.

When He Steals Your Soul

122

Inner children are not the only pieces of vital energy that can be brought back from soul retrieval and working with lost pieces. We can experience soul loss at any stage of our lives for a variety of reasons.

One common experience for adults is experiencing soul loss in familial and romantic relationships. While relationships are amazing teachers and catalysts in our emotional and spiritual lives, they often involve a lot of trauma. When we are abandoned by our partners or cheated on, we may experience soul loss. When we willingly give up our power for our partner, we may experience soul loss. When a marriage grows apart and ends in a bittersweet fashion, we may experience soul loss. Sometimes the other person will want to keep the vital energy they stole or were given, and they won't want to give it up.

Tara was in an abusive relationship with a man she believed to be very spiritually powerful. His power was what first attracted her to him, as she was interested in spiritual studies but didn't believe she had her own power. She willingly gave her power to him in the beginning as a show of adoration, but as the relationship progressed, she realized she couldn't get it back. She was trapped in the pull of him as he continued to be abusive toward her.

As I facilitated a soul retrieval session with her, I discovered that I needed to retrieve that piece of vital energy from her abusive partner, who still held it closely. In what can only be described as a negotiation/battle, I was able to take that energy from him so I could return it to its rightful owner, Tara.

In the moment I returned Tara's missing energy to her body, she jumped. She could feel that something had returned, and she felt fuller. She felt a sense of power and security she had been lacking, and upon integrating that energy, no longer felt the need to give her power to others.

There are likely relationships in your past that you can already identify as sources of soul loss. You may know exactly when and where that soul loss occurred. Getting back that vital piece of energy is a lot safer and more effective when you see a professional healer.

123

Should You Stay or Should You Go?

Empaths who venture down this road of self-discovery are often at a crossroads in their life regarding their relationships. They are usually growing apart from their partner as they begin to realize what it means for them to be an empath. Relationships are often our greatest teachers, and many times, those teachers aren't meant to stick around in our lives forever.

Your choice in your mate is one of the most important factors in your life, since this person will share physical and energetic space with you on a regular basis. This person will affect how you work with your boundaries, how you express your feelings, how safe you feel when vulnerable, and how connected you are with your higher self.

Part of doing the intense self-work of the empath is letting go of relationships that cause you to struggle with your boundaries, safety, and vulnerability. Whether it's a marriage of twenty years that has no room for growth or change, or an intense relationship of two years that has been a catalyst of self-exploration and realization but has brought you to different paths, relationships ebb and flow, and sometimes the tide pulls us away from them for good.

As overwhelmed empaths, we are typically drawn to relationships where we are the primary nurturers and caretakers of the relationship. The emotional labor falls to us to keep the relationship stable, so when an empath comes into their empowerment and independence, their partner may not be so keen to give up the extra emotional space they've been able to occupy with them before. Giving up that womb space is scary for them, and they may not support your growth because of that fear. For empaths who no longer want to be overwhelmed, this lack of support is a major cause for relationships ending.

A lot of shame comes with breaking up, especially if it's a marriage. We tend to label these "failed relationships," but I don't believe any relationship that was created out of love can ever be a failure. When a relationship ends, it's because one or both people grew so much that the relationship was no longer a suitable container for them. In that way, the ending of a relationship is a positive thing, a herald of exciting things to come. If you're lucky, you may have a partner who's willing and able to grow and evolve at the same rate that you grow and evolve or, at the very least, support you in your own growth in a way that doesn't take away from the relationship.

Deciding when to stay and when to go is never easy for the empath with the big heart. Saying goodbye to loved ones is a loss. To become the person you want to become, you will undoubtedly lose things. Whether it's romantic relationships, places, friends, or jobs, the road to empowered empathy is paved with some grief.

That grief, as painful as it may be, will give you the clarity and wisdom to appreciate your truest self and your truest mission. If you must go, the person on the other side of that loss, the person you want to become, is waiting for you, and they have so many wonderful things they want to show you.

DO THE WORK 125

Exploring energetic patterns will help you develop relationships that are healthier for you and the other. Use the exercises here to discover more about the patterns that hold you back.

Energetic Pattern Inventory

Take an inventory of your most important relationships. Start with one relationship, but do this with every key relationship. You can even do this with past relationships to examine the pattern.

- Do you become a chameleon in this relationship? Do you change yourself to accommodate the emotional needs of the other person? If so, in what ways?

- Do you use the concept of unconditional love to excuse the lack of boundaries in this relationship? If so, what are the circumstances?

- Do you have a codependent relationship with this person? Does your happiness rely heavily on what they think of you?

- Does the other person emotionally abuse you or gaslight you in any way? Do you feel like they are the ones telling you what your feelings mean?

- Do you find that the other person shows signs of narcissism, manipulating your empathy? Do *you* show signs of narcissism, manipulating *their* empathy?

- *Do you feel like this relationship allows you to grow? Does it support the changes you make in your life?*

You may notice that the patterns you experience the most are linked to your core wounds. We often find ways to replay our core wounding through our relationships when we haven't yet faced those core wounds. Once you begin to notice these patterns in your own relationships, it becomes easier and easier to stop them in their tracks and break the cycle.

The Victim and Villain in Your Relationships

Pick an important relationship in your life right now. In your journal, make a list of the last three fights the two of you had. Describe the circumstances that led up to the fight, what you both said, how you felt. Think back to your descriptions of your victim and your villain. Can you see either of them in your fight? Can you see your victim shutting down and blaming the other person? Can you see your villain manipulating the other person, or saying cruel things? Where do you see your victim or villain acting out in this fight? Do this for each fight, and see if you can notice a pattern. Your victim and your villain, as well as the victim and villain of your loved one, are pretty predictable. They most reliably come out when they've been triggered in an argument. By shedding light on the behaviors of your victim and villain, you're also shedding light on the common energetic patterns you run as a default when you're feeling threatened or scared. When you see the patterns and get to know them, you can more easily change them.

CHAPTER 8

Working Through Trauma

As I walked the shoreline in Aberdeen, Scotland, my eyes alternated between getting lost in the vast misty horizon of the North Sea and searching the pebbles beneath my feet as the waves rushed in to meet them. I was looking for sea glass. Glancing forward, glints of blue and green would catch my eye, shining from a fresh wave. I collected the pieces of softened glass like they were pieces of lost treasure. I washed them with the utmost of care, appreciating each one, wondering what they had been before, and how long they had been in the sea.

My love of sea glass extended far past a physical appreciation. To me, sea glass is the most beautiful example of the resiliency of brokenness. What starts as a million tiny particles of sand being formed into a cohesive shape by extreme heat, is then eventually shattered again, losing its form. It is tossed in all directions, worn by years of constant waves, softened, and made into something completely different but still beautiful. At any point, it could be shattered again or formed into something else entirely. And no matter its current state, it will never erase the glory of former incarnations, and it will never erase the trauma of being shattered. No matter its current state, it's both completely broken and completely whole all at once.

One of the hardest aspects of being an empath is working with all of the pain that comes with it—the brokenness of living a human life, the trauma from past experiences, the things that get in our way when we're feeling it all. The best way to work with it is to lean into it rather than away from it. To do this, you embrace your brokenness, communicate with your trauma, and discover ways to work through your obstacles.

130

We Are Both Broken and Whole

I am broken.

I know that saying this is a spiritual no-no.

But there it is: I am broken.

You're broken, too, though.

I can't tell you how many times I've seen the affirmation *I am whole* used by spiritual mentors and gurus, or how many times I've spoken about my brokenness to be met with something like "No, you've never been broken. You are whole and perfect just the way you are."

It's a nice thing to think, that someone is whole and perfect just the way they are. Though the intention is good and the goal is to move toward positive thinking, this affirmation is another one of those new age distortions.

Have you ever told someone who is deeply suffering that they are whole and perfect just the way they are? Imagine telling a rape survivor that they are whole, and that their rape did not break them, that their rape is part of what makes them perfect. Imagine telling a mother grieving the loss of her child that she is not broken, and that her grief is part of what makes her perfect and whole. By telling *anyone*, whether you know their personal pain or not, that they are whole and perfect, you are unconsciously telling them that they deserve their pain and their trauma. You are telling them that the horrific injustices of the world are part of a perfect reality, *their* perfect reality. You are invalidating their life experience.

One night, I was sitting on my bed with my five-year-old rescue dog, Nimue. I adopted her when she was almost one, and she had come from a mysterious abusive situation where she was kept locked in a garage and starved. I noticed a fly in the room with us and stood up, grabbing a roll of paper towels to smack it. As I raised my arm above my head, Nimue put her

131

ears back and jumped off the bed, cowering from me. I had accidentally triggered her abuse by raising my arm near her. I immediately dropped my arm and called her back onto the bed, hugging her and kissing her and whispering calming things in her ear.

"I love you," I cooed to her as I petted her head, "I would never hurt you."

Even though she hadn't been harmed in the four years I'd had her, even though she received an abundance of love, snuggles, treats, and play, the first year of her life was so painful that it still affected her. It was so painful that it would probably affect her for the rest of her life, regardless of the love she received. In that moment, holding her in my arms and crying a few silent tears for her, I realized that she was broken in the same way I was broken—in the same way many of us are broken, and always will be.

132   Living in a world where terrible things can and do happen undeniably breaks us. Living in a world where we experience soul-shattering pain and loss undeniably breaks us. Living in a world where the ones we trust hurt and abuse us undeniably breaks us. Let's stop pretending we're not broken. Just like you wouldn't pick up a piece of sea glass and think, *Look! I found a whole bottle that has never been broken before,* you wouldn't pick up the painful experience of a person and insist that they are whole.

This isn't to say we can't *also* be whole, but as human beings living human lives, we cannot be whole without also being broken. In the empath's quest for personal power and validation, the definition of *wholeness* must be changed from something that is perfect and good to something that is merely complete. True wholeness includes the entire spectrum of experience, from the positive and uplifting to the damning and heartbreaking. And if your life experience has some pain mixed in (which it undoubtedly does if you're really a human), your own wholeness must include the acceptance of your brokenness.

What Is Trauma?

On your journey to wholeness, you have to know the trauma that you're dealing with. With respect to energetics, *trauma* is an experience that causes a psychological injury or energetic wound. When you experience trauma, your nervous system and adrenals are lit up in fight, flight, or freeze mode, and that adrenaline and fear is absorbed into the cells in your body, creating an energy signature that lives inside your body and aura. When we work with trauma on an energetic level, keep in mind that the energy is inextricably tied to your body. Your body remembers your trauma even when your conscious mind has forgotten.

133

Empaths and Their Relationship to Trauma

For an empath, traumatic experiences can be magnified. Because empaths experience pain so much more intensely, trauma can be an incredibly visceral experience. A seemingly small slight can create trauma much bigger than you'd think. Your core wounds are an excellent example of this. Even if your core wound was a relatively benign event (like me with the dead bird), for a highly sensitive person, it can feel impossibly overwhelming and large, which is how it creates that foundation of emotional pain. These trauma events may be so painful and dangerous to the empath that soul loss occurs in order for them to survive. This is when soul retrieval is needed for those split selves.

Not only do empaths absorb their fair share of their own trauma, but they often absorb the trauma of others. Empaths are trauma collectors. Not only do many of us have storied pasts filled with pain and abuse, but we also collect trauma from the stories of others. Trauma seems to cozy itself right into the curves of our bodies and the cracks in our minds. We inherit it from our grandmothers and their grandmothers before them. Our natural openness and compassion, plus the influence of our boundaries (or lack thereof), make us the perfect candidates to be energetic unloading zones.

Scientific studies show how trauma in our family can pass down through generations, affecting younger family members with the same trauma the older members experienced. This phenomenon explains why we often inherit the same problems as our relatives who came before us. The problems may manifest in different ways, but they often have the same theme or root.

This is why daughters are often afflicted with the same abusive relationships their mothers endured, or why sons have the same violent fear of abandonment their fathers do. We can find these themes in our own spiritual and emotional DNA as we do the shadow work of identifying and consciously working with those feelings and tracing them back to their roots. We can't help but find ourselves in those same patterns as our parents.

We learn how to carry both our own trauma and that of others. We adjust to it. We become trauma-management systems rather than trauma-clearing systems. Usually this way of living is learned very early on. By the time we're adults, we often don't realize how much trauma we're actually carrying until we are so subconsciously loaded that a simple trigger can initiate a domino effect in the psyche, carrying us to an involuntary breaking point.

Time to Face Your Trauma

If you've been carrying around your trauma on your own, pushing it down so you can survive, a huge part of your work as an empath will be to identify and start working with it. Maybe you've put on a brave face, showing the world how strong you are to be able to handle all of this.

But none of us can be strong all the time. None of us can always have our act together. When you keep pushing past traumatic or stressful events, when you keep telling yourself it will all be fine as long as you keep hustling past it, the trauma slowly builds up in your system. While in that forced-strength mindset, you may find yourself in even more traumatizing or stressful situations. You may say, "Oh, I'm strong. I can handle this. This is fine."

But it's *not* fine. It's not fine to push yourself past your limits with declarations of your fine-ness. It's not fine to shove your trauma down, thinking you'll be able to pull it out in small pieces later, but only when you're ready. Trauma doesn't work that way. If you disrespect your trauma, it may very well swallow you whole.

135

The less we listen to what our trauma needs to heal, the more likely we are to unintentionally retraumatize ourselves, sending ourselves into unhealthy and dangerous cycles of behavior and thought patterns. Our stubbornness to be fierce and powerful all the time can end up hurting us if we don't take the steps to stop, listen, and heal.

The good news is that your trauma always wants to talk to you and to tell you what it needs. It will tell you when it's time to bravely come forward, and it will tell you when it's time to hold back and nurture your raw nerves.

None of us are excluded from dealing with trauma. We all have accumulated trauma throughout our lives, both from our own experiences and the experiences of others. Having trauma doesn't mean you're screwed up beyond repair or you're abnormal in some way. Trauma is a very normal part of life—a part that should be encountered with as much compassion and awareness as possible.

Facing your own trauma affects the trauma of your family lineage as well. When you do this type of transformative emotional work on yourself, your entire ancestral line before you and after you benefits from that work. By healing yourself and sifting through your own trauma and karma, you assist in healing your mother's karma and your grandmother's karma and on and on. You also assist in healing your daughter's karma and your granddaughter's karma and on and on. Sometimes, when you embark on a healing journey, members of your family want to join in the healing, and that has even more of a ripple effect in your lineage. Other times, your family will want nothing to do with your healing, and that's okay too. They will still benefit from your own work in some way, even if you don't have a close relationship. If your relationship with your family is a struggle, and one that's not likely to change in their lifetimes, you are still providing new patterning for your children and their children. You are still breaking the cycle of trauma.

Identify Your Traumas

You've already done a lot of work in identifying your traumas. You've done this when working with your core wounds and triggers. Have you noticed that certain parts of this work have been harder to deal with than others? Were there some exercises that brought up more pain than others? Now is the time to create some more space for those tough-to-digest feelings of trauma. In the Do the Work section of this chapter, you'll have the opportunity to identify and revisit those.

Creating Safe Spaces for Trauma

By doing this kind of emotional digging, a lot of old trauma can surface. That trauma needs a safe space to exist. A *safe space* is an emotional container that's free of judgment and which allows your experience to unfold naturally. For your safe space, first create the actual physical environment. Go somewhere you feel protected and comfortable. Get away from people who don't understand what you're doing. When you create a physical environment to protect the trauma that comes up, you automatically set a precedent—that it's okay to feel your feelings.

Next, limit your trauma exposure while in your safe space. Even though you are setting yourself up to experience your triggers and your trauma, you don't have to experience more trauma and triggers than you're prepared to handle. Knowing your limits is crucial. Emotional work is hard and it really opens you up, which makes you much more raw and vulnerable than usual. Don't think that you always have to face your trauma head-on in the boldest way possible. You're a beautiful, sensitive being, and sometimes you need time to face it with courage. If triggers of your trauma are simply too much to handle, attempting to face them head-on may actually retraumatize you.

137

If you're working through the trauma of being physically assaulted, avoid watching violent movies and TV shows. If you're working through the anxiety of your trauma, avoid large crowds or situations that you know will trigger that anxiety. If you're working through the trauma of rape, stay away from those pop-BDSM books. Get off social media for a bit. You don't need to be exposed to similar trauma as you're processing the initial trauma.

There is no shame in avoiding known triggers to your trauma. You need to take care of yourself, and that often means you need to be extra sensitive to and protective of your vulnerability. It's okay to avoid situations that you know trigger you. It's okay to avoid places, people, or activities that could potentially retraumatize you. Forcing yourself into a stressful or traumatizing situation is not strength—it's disrespect. You don't have to prove to yourself or anyone else what you can handle. You don't have to prove to yourself or anyone else that you're an indestructible force of nature or that you're "overcoming" your trauma. It's important to remember that you don't simply "overcome" your trauma. You develop a relationship with it, a loving understanding of it, and then it plays less and less of a role in your life as a result. Your safe space should be free of expectations like overcoming trauma or being strong. In your safe space, you're allowed to simply exist in your feelings, however they want to show up.

Your next step is to do some focused work with your trauma. Exercises like journaling, personifying your feelings, tracing your triggers back, and having conscious pity parties can help you work through some of that trauma while in that safe space. Letting yourself grieve is an important step, since our trauma is often pushed down to the extent that we may not even realize its depth. Screaming and crying for three straight days might be just what your trauma needs. Writing a book about your experience could be just what your trauma needs. Whatever you can do to feel that grief and express it safely is what you need to do. Since trauma changes you, you may need to mourn a version of yourself that you once were, or that you cannot be, when you're working with your grief. In the Do the Work section of this chapter, an exercise will help you process this kind of grief.

It's important to know that, even if you have your own safe space, you may need additional support. None of us can be strong and capable all of the time, especially when working with our own trauma. Sometimes the grief is too strong and the feelings are too real, and we can't do it on our own. Sometimes we have to know what our limits are for going it alone.

If the trauma is too much, there is no shame in seeking support. Whether that support looks like staying with your mom for a few days, working with a healer, or seeking medical attention, all support is good support. Trauma and grief are difficult and complex processes, and it's natural to feel completely destabilized by it all. If you have a history of complex trauma, or prolonged or multiple traumatic events, it's even more important to have extra support, since that's harder to deal with on your own. It's always a good thing to find support in whatever way you can, whether you call a compassionate friend or you pay an amazing healer or therapist to hold the space for you.

When you go through this kind of emotional work, you allow yourself to be a caterpillar in a cocoon. Inside, you've broken down into a big pile of conscious goo, and you need that cocoon to protect you while you're so vulnerable. Having that cocoon in the form of supportive people and a dedicated safe space will help you become the gorgeous butterfly that you really are.

139

Feeling Is Healing

Pulling up so much of your past pain can be jarring to your system. If you've been repressing so much of your pain for so long, that pain will rage as it rises up to be validated and cleansed. This emotional work actually causes energetic healing, and as that healing takes place, it pushes out the old pain you don't need anymore. When it's being pushed out, you have to *feel* it being pushed out. All of those raw emotions that clutched your pain are being released, but you will feel the intensity and purity of those raw emotions. If you release a lot of rage, you'll *feel* that rage coming out as if it were brand-new. Because you're an empath, and emotions are magnified for you, that rage will feel even stronger and sharper.

If you feel rage, allow yourself to feel the rage fully. Releasing your pain is uncomfortable, but it has to be done, and just because you feel those emotions are out of control, that doesn't mean you're not on the right track. It doesn't mean you're going insane. It doesn't mean you've lost all your progress. It means you're exactly on track, you're doing the right things, and you have to let these things pass through.

This process can last longer if you're releasing a lot, and it can often feel like you're stuck in the grieving of the emotion and you can't get out. But this part is not forever.

This part is the necessary mess of healing. Healing is not a pretty process, contrary to what gurus may tell you. Healing is brutal and honest and raw and destructive. There is a beauty in that destruction, but it's not easy and it's not calm. Know that this part will pass, even if you feel overwhelmed by those emotions.

This emotional storm will pass, and you'll be surprised to find how calm you are on the other side of it.

140

Integrating Trauma

It might be difficult to imagine a life without latent trauma causing all sorts of problems. Integrating trauma is rarely easy, as it requires so much work, attention, and vulnerability. After doing any emotional work on your trauma—whether it was identifying it, energetically feeling it, or expressing it in a sacred way—*time* for integration is needed.

Energetic integration is fairly simple in what it needs: lots of water, rest, and permission. It needs to cry when it feels like it; it needs to laugh when it feels like it; it needs to sleep as much as possible. You may even find yourself hungrier than usual after some intense emotional work, as the food you eat can help ground you during integration. Being gentle with yourself is necessary, especially since you may have a lot of different feelings popping up unexpectedly at different times. Allowing the feelings to flow through you will ease the integration and will naturally lead you into the next phase of integration, which is likely more water and more sleep. Because you're especially sensitive to the energies of others as an empath, it's also important to make sure you're getting enough alone time so that your process isn't being confused by too many other energies.

Integrating our trauma doesn't mean we rid ourselves of it. It doesn't mean we've defeated it or destroyed it or will never have to deal with it again. Integrating it means that it won't run our lives anymore, and that we can use it to better understand ourselves and the way we see the world. Integrating it helps us express our stories in a sacred way, without losing power to them. Integrating your trauma will actually give you more personal power in the world.

There is a Japanese art known as Kintsugi, in which broken pottery is repaired using a special lacquer dusted with powdered gold. This process gives the repaired item seams of shining gold, emphasizing the places where it was once broken. Kintsugi translates to "golden joinery," and its alternate name, Kintsukuroi, translates to "golden repair." The Japanese believe that items which have been broken are more interesting, and that their brokenness offers a beautiful history of the item. Repairing such a piece with gold shows a respect and an appreciation of that history, without the need to hide or

141

disguise it. Many would agree that these items are far more beautiful and unique after having been broken.

Kintsugi is an amazing physical reflection of how to integrate trauma. Imagine how much better the world would be if we could all treat our trauma and brokenness the way Kintsugi treats pottery. What if we didn't have to hide the places where trauma has broken us? If we could see the beauty in the places we've been broken, call back those broken pieces with love, and use gold to repair ourselves, the voices and stories and histories in this life would be astonishing, life-affirming, and incredibly healing. What if we emphasized our own broken history to make our life more beautiful?

Most amazing causes are borne out of the pain of brokenness and trauma. Foundations are started by those who have lost loved ones to diseases and suffering. Movements are started by those who have been afflicted by injustice. Stories are written and songs are sung by those who cannot contain the pain inside themselves any longer. As Rumi said, "The wound is where the light enters."

Integrating your trauma is like letting the light enter. It's the practice of loving all your broken pieces and fusing them together with love, support, and community.

DO THE WORK

Working through your trauma allows you to move more fully and freely into your life. These exercises will help you process your pain.

Name Your Pain

Look back on all the exercises you've done so far. Look at your core wounds, your victim and your villain, your energy signatures, your triggers. Remember which ones were the most difficult for you. Was there a certain practice that felt much heavier than the others? Make a note of which parts were the hardest for you to process.

Each of those exercises was tied to experiences in your life. Allow yourself to remember the experiences that made those practices so difficult. Make a list of those life experiences. This is where your trauma is.

Mourn Yourself

Trauma changes us. Because we don't ask for the trauma, it can be really hard to accept those changes. You may struggle to hold on to an idea of a person that doesn't fit you anymore, a person that you can't **be** anymore. If you hold on to these ideas of the person you can't be because of your trauma, you will start to feel like a ghost in your own body. Acknowledging and crying over this person that you cannot be will help you move forward with who you actually are. These old versions of yourself as well as the **desired** versions of yourself that never came to pass need to die so that you can live in the present.

143

In your journal, write an obituary for the aspect of yourself that cannot be. Allow yourself the space to mourn yourself—the you that cannot be.

Epilogue

If you've read this far, you should feel incredibly proud of yourself. You've conquered what very few people will attempt in their lifetime. You have faced yourself and have reclaimed the power that facing yourself entails.

You've examined what it means to be an empath. You've flipped the script to focus on who you are for *yourself*, instead of just who you are for other people. You've approached your brokenness, your shadow side, and your inner child with open eyes and an open heart. You've built up your energy signatures and learned what messages your feelings bring you. You've learned to differentiate between your own energy and the energy of others, and you've used that knowledge to cleanse yourself of the energy that's not yours. You've realized your boundaries are always in their perfect place, and you've learned how to communicate with your intuition to find and fine-tune those boundaries. You've seen the energetic patterns in your relationships and how they connect to your core wounds.

Most of all, you've learned to harness the power of the darkness that is your shadow side. All of those intense emotional ups and downs have revealed a source of clarity and stability in your own practice and your own growth. This kind of awareness will follow you for the rest of your life, and you will be able to handle your emotions and your relationships with a grace you never thought possible.

Knowing yourself this well creates solid stability in your abilities. Knowing yourself this well prevents others from messing with that stability. Knowing yourself this well means that no one will ever be able to take your power away.

My wish for you is that you go out there and show up in the world in a new way. You have a unique set of skills no one else possesses, and that's what will change the world. My wish for you is that you'll never stand in your own way again and that you will do what you came here to do. Whether you're a healer, a teacher, a channeler, a parent, an activist, a friend, you can only be a force of unbelievable power and strength now. Owning and reclaiming all of the power that comes from integrating your darkness will change you and the lives of everyone around you.

Know that you can come back to this work and these practices for the rest of your life. Your energy will shift and change as you grow, and so the work will shift and change as well.

While you can't make yourself *not* be an empath anymore, you can see how your life can change when you work with it rather than against it. Where you were once overwhelmed by everyone else's energy, you can now sort it out, creating space for yourself. Where you were once frustrated with all the complexities in your relationships, you can now see the energetic patterns you're a part of and decide to alter them or cut them off altogether.

You're in control of your own life.

And I can't wait to see what you do with it.

Resources

Energetics 101

For an empath, everything begins and ends with energy. If you are sensitive to other people and their feelings, what you're actually sensitive to is energy. Energy affects us on all levels: emotional, physical, psychological, spiritual. Each level has its own way of processing and reacting to energy, which is why it's so important to figure out the way *you* receive and process energy. Every emotion has an energy, and energy is constantly moving and changing. Anger is an energy. Love is an energy. When someone expresses anger or love, what they're really doing is experiencing the energy of anger and love, and trying to find ways to share what they're feeling. You know when you step into a room, and you get strange vibes from it? Or when you walk into a crowd and you suddenly feel overwhelmed? That's because you're feeling energy. You may feel strange vibes from an empty room because of the energy that's left from whomever was in it before. You may feel overwhelmed in a crowd because you're feeling the energy of everyone in the crowd.

Empaths are like barometers for energy. You can pick up on and read the energetic influences around you. You're also reading the energetic influences within yourself at the same time. This explains why it can become really confusing or overwhelming for an empath to figure out whose energy is whose. And since you can't control the way that others put out energy around you, it's especially important to control the way that *you* handle your own energy.

One way you can start working with your energy is by working with your chakras. *Chakras* are spinning wheels of energy in your body that are always working and processing energy. There are seven primary chakras.

The root chakra is located at the base of your spine. Its color is red. This chakra works with your basic instincts— your physical survival and your primary drives of hunger, thirst, sex, and safety. This chakra rules passion, anger, lust, and the fight-or-flight response.

Your second chakra, the sacral chakra, is located just below the naval. Its color is orange. This chakra works with your emotional well-being. This chakra is one of the most important chakras to work with when diving into empath shadow work. Here you'll find the primary center for your emotions and how you process them.

Your third chakra, the solar plexus chakra, is located above your naval and below your rib cage, where your diaphragm rests. Its color is yellow. This chakra rules your willpower, your vitality, and your ability to confidently make decisions.

Your fourth chakra, your heart chakra, is located right in the center of your chest. Its color is green. Pale pink is also a heart chakra color. Your heart chakra rules your capacity for love, forgiveness, and compassion.

Your fifth chakra, your throat chakra, is located in the center of your throat. Its color is blue. This chakra rules your ability to speak your truth and use your voice.

Your sixth chakra, your third-eye chakra, is located in the center of your forehead. Its color is indigo, and this chakra rules your intuition.

Your seventh chakra, your crown chakra, is located at the top of your head. Its color is violet (or white), and this chakra rules your connection to higher powers.

All of your chakras work in harmony to balance your energy, but since they're constantly processing energy, it's easy for them to become unbalanced. Blockages in your chakras will make your experience of energy (and your experience of life) a little harder. For example, if you have a blockage in your throat chakra, you may have a hard time sticking up for yourself. You may find it difficult to use your voice in situations where you need to. By working on your throat chakra, you can clear out that energy blockage and find your strength in your voice.

It's easy to work with your chakras. You can use guided meditations and color visualization. You can use stones that are the same color as the chakra you're working on. As a general guideline, your higher chakras (your third-eye chakra and especially your crown chakra) need a much lighter touch than your lower chakras. They don't need as much interaction and focused work as your lower chakras do. Your higher chakras work primarily with heavenly energies and don't need the same amount of human intervention. Your lower chakras work primarily with earthly energies, so they are much easier to work with on your own, and can handle a lot more focused work than your higher chakras.

149

Because of your sensitivity to energy, you may experience physical symptoms in the chakra that the energy or emotion is in. Although it can be annoying, feeling those symptoms can indicate where your blockages are, and where you need to focus your healing efforts.

As always, if you're overwhelmed by the thought of working with your own energy, turn to a trusted healing practitioner or teacher by talking to your community and doing your research.

Energetic Clearing Tools

When I graduated college, I took a mystical journey out West. I rode the train from Minneapolis, Minnesota, to Portland, Oregon. On the train ride there, however, the train got stuck in the middle of the mountains in Montana. We sat on the tracks for hours—miles from civilization, no cell service, in the midst of the wilds of Glacier National Park. I sat in the observation car, the mountains looming over me, a taunting cliffside below me. All I could see were trees and rocks, height and depth, in every direction. The sun was shining through the pines. The sky was bluer than blue. It was the most beautiful thing I had ever seen.

And yet, I panicked. This was the first time I had been so disconnected, so out of reach, from the people and places I'd left behind. Knowing I couldn't reach anyone I knew, even if I wanted to, amplified my panic.

Here I was, facing the wild unknown, the overpowering and overwhelming beauty and terror of nature, and I suddenly felt as though I didn't exist. How could I exist in the mountains? I was small and alone. And I realized that as emotionally isolated as I'd felt my entire life, I'd never felt *that* energetically and physically alone. I'd never felt so free from the cords of others. And it scared me because being empty and nonexistent in the trees was so new, so uncharted, so wild. I had grown accustomed to having all those energetic cords with other people, and the idea of being without them was terrifying. I would soon learn that this was the reason that nature is such powerful medicine.

For an empath, nature strips away all the pretenses, all the energetic cords, all the codependency and the obligation, and allows one to simply be nonexistent. To simply *be*. Without everything else. But even though it is medicine, it's still scary. Being truly alone forces the empath to question their entire identity and reason for existing. It challenges the inherent belief that an empath exists for others, and begs the question, "Who are you when everyone else is gone?"

The answer to that question is exactly what we're looking for, and it's something we can't answer until we've cleared ourselves of everyone else's energy.

Having a set of energetic clearing practices is a must for any empath. Being able to clear out stagnant or excess energy will make room for the bigger questions the empath must face: Who am I *really*? What is my purpose?

If you're constantly bombarded by the energy of everyone else, you won't get the opportunity to explore your own identity because you'll be too busy managing their feelings and energies. To prevent that from happening, you need a regular routine of clearing and maintenance. Here are some of the most effective tools for energetic clearing. Try them all and see which you'd like to work into your normal routine.

Give Yourself Some Space

One of the easiest ways to clear energy is to get some space. It's so much harder to clear out other people's energies when you're still actually with them. Creating physical separation from those people starts the untangling process.

Go to your family cabin alone. Check in to a hotel room by yourself. Stay at a friend's farmhouse. Getting physical space sets the stage for you to sort through your feelings safely. Using nature as a tool will speed up the process of clearing.

If you aren't able to fully get away, creating a space in your home for your use only will work too. Claim the guest room for yourself for a while. Set up an altar in your bedroom. Tell your family they're not allowed to bother you when you're in that space.

Make this space sacred by creating a little altar for yourself. Put things you treasure and find special on this altar. It could be your favorite stones, a picture of your grandmother, leaves you gathered from the woods, animal figurines, your favorite gemstone jewelry or oracle deck, or other things that are important to you. Altars are made even more powerful if you can represent each element on them. For earth, you can use a stone or a stick. For air, a feather, or burning incense. For water, a seashell or an actual vial of water from your favorite place. (I have a bottle of water from Lake Superior on my altar.) For fire, a lit candle.

Claiming space just for yourself, and treating this space as sacred, will naturally set you up for processing and cleansing.

Turn to Nature

Nature is the easiest tool you can use that will bring you directly into the true reality of being an empath: the wild emptiness of creation, the void. Nature cuts your energetic cords. It doesn't ask you to manage its energy, it doesn't ask you to take on its emotions. Because the energy of nature is mostly neutral, it doesn't push and pull your energy the way that other people do. Its neutrality is healing. Getting away from others and into nature will quickly encourage you to examine your own energy instead of burying it in the feelings of others. Nature will see and nurture you and all your feelings in a way that other humans can't. Turning to nature may sometimes feel like running away, but it's not. It's giving your

152

soul a chance to hit the refresh button, and giving you a chance to connect to yourself without risking the interference of others.

Smoke Cleansing

Smoke cleansing is the act of purifying energy by burning certain plant materials. The most commonly used material for smoke cleansing is white sage. Burning bundles or leaves of white sage creates a strong herbal odor and cleanses the area of heavy and dense energies.

Another common option is palo santo wood, which comes from fallen trees in South America and gives off a sweet and smoky scent, like resin and campfire. Palo santo works wonderfully in conjunction with white sage, as the sage is best at purifying, while the palo santo is best at bringing down additional positive energies.

There are many other options, like cedar, frankincense, sweetgrass, lavender, mugwort, and pine. Nag Champa incense is also good for transmuting energy. You'll discover your own favorites. Using herbs from sustainable and respectful sources is always good, both for the respect of the process and also the respect of the earth.

153

Use smoke cleansing as often as you like. Smoke cleansing can help shift the energy after an argument or a bad experience. If you've just had a fight with your partner, cleanse. If you just hosted a family dinner that was like pulling teeth, cleanse. If you woke up from a bad dream, cleanse. If you're feeling like a bitch for no reason, cleanse. Clearing out those excess energies will help you feel calmer and clearer, and it will help you be able to identify what is *your* energy by noticing what sticks around afterward.

Rituals

Using rituals and prayers is another way to clear out the energy of others and release your own blockages. There are many options for doing this, but I'm going to give you a few of my favorites that will be easy to work into your routine.

ARCHANGEL MICHAEL CLEARING

(Recite this clearing out loud.)

I invoke Archangel Michael with the fifth dimensional tube of light.
Michael, please place this tube of light around me
in this lifetime and all lifetimes,
all planetary systems and all solar systems,
all alternate realities and all parallel realities,
all alternate universes and all parallel universes,
as well as all source systems,
in this time and in all times.
Michael, use your sword of light to clear me of all foreign energies,
all thought forms and beings, and when I am clear,
escort these energies into the tube of light,
and return them to the fifth dimension
to be transmuted to another form of light.
Close up my aura to the influences of all beings,
except of my higher self, the God consciousness,
my guides and guardians.
So be it, and so it is.

You may notice that you feel physical sensations after you've recited this. I always feel a rush of heat around me, as if

I can actually feel the tube of light clearing me. You may feel something similar, or you may also feel a slight sense of panic if you're attached to your cords. The act of clearing out our cords can be scary, since we're so used to having them.

If you recite this clearing three times and find that you still feel a heavy negative feeling, that means the feeling you're experiencing is yours. This isn't a bad thing, though, as it informs you where you need to turn your attention.

FULL MOON RELEASING

The full moon is the perfect time to release the things that no longer serve you.

On the night of the full moon, write a list of everything you're ready to purge. Really put your intention into writing this list, and feel each thing as you're writing it. Offer your list to the moon, reciting each thing out loud and offering a dedication.

Your dedication will sound something like this (though you can create your own however you wish):

Lady Luna, Glorious Moon,
I offer up my grievances,
and all of the things that don't serve me anymore.
I ask for your assistance in taking these things
and transmuting them with your power
for my highest good.
So be it [or *Amen*].

Burn your list, whether it's over a bonfire, in a candle flame, or in a burning bowl. If you use a burning bowl, sprinkle the ashes on the ground outside (or bury them, if you prefer), and thank the earth for taking these things.

155

Crystals and Stones

Crystals and stones are a fun way to employ more energetic tools in your life. Each crystal has its own specific spiritual energy, and using those energies in your meditations, your healings, and as decorations throughout your home, will bring in some additional transformation energy.

There's a wealth of knowledge online about each crystal and its properties, and most new age shops or gem shops have little cards that give you information as well. Picking a crystal that you're drawn to, even before knowing what that crystal does, is a fun form of divination as well.

I couldn't even begin to list all the crystals and their properties, but I'll list a few of the most commonly used ones.

Amethyst: A purple stone used for psychic work and intuition development. Works with the third-eye chakra and the crown chakra.

Citrine: An orange stone used for emotional work and willpower. Works with the sacral chakra and solar plexus.

Lapis Lazuli: A blue stone used for work with self-expression and truth. Works with the throat chakra.

Quartz: A white/clear stone that's used for amplifying and purifying energy. Works with all the chakras.

Rose Quartz: A pink stone used for self-love and romantic love. Works with the heart chakra.

Tourmaline: A black stone used for protection and grounding. Works with the root chakra, but also all of them.

Try putting your favorite stone on its corresponding chakra while you meditate! Look for a stone that's good for whatever aspect you want to work on. Have fun with it, because crystals are a beautiful thing to have around your sacred space.

Reminders

Any physical reminder of the emotional work you do will strengthen that work. Inner work is very heavy, and most of it goes completely unseen by the outside world. Having little physical reminders of the work you're doing will keep you connected and validate your work.

If you recently had a powerful meditation featuring a deer, find a little deer figurine to set out on your altar. Write down your favorite pain alchemy affirmation and tape it on your mirror. If your inner child wants to color, have your coloring books out on your coffee table as a reminder. These practices will help keep your energy clear.

157

Play Around

To know which tools work the best for you, you have to play around with your options. Your intuition may lead you to your favorite one right away, or you may find that the one you least expected is actually the most effective for you. You may also find or create your own tools for cleansing your energy. Start small and take the pieces you're ready for while leaving the rest.

Acknowledgments

A huge thank you to Katzi, Kathleen, and Kim for journeying down this path with me. Your experiences and insights were invaluable to the writing process, and I have been constantly in awe of your honesty, your courage, and your raw power. You each have taught me so much. I will forever have a place in my heart for my divine "K" women.

To Dr. Angela Lauria, thank you for being the badass coach that you are and for demanding the clearest and purest messages from my book and my practice. You saw me in a place I didn't yet see myself, and what I've learned from you has created a powerful foundation I will continue to build upon for the rest of my life.

Thank you, Erin Schroeder, for the endless hours of girl talk on discernment, shadow work, messed up industries, social justice, sisterhood, and how to *really* grow and evolve as a lightworker and friend. You're a daily inspiration for me, and I'm proud to be your friend.

I'm also grateful for all of the teachers, healers, and peers I've worked with in my decade of spiritual exploration and healing. I've learned so much about both the light and the shadows, and, since they've brought me to this point, I wouldn't change my experiences one bit.

Thank you to the team at New Harbinger Publications for shaping my book into something incredible and bringing it into the world in a big way!

Ora North is an empath and healer who grew tired of the "love and light" scene. She felt a lack of authenticity in the new age movement and turned to emotional shadow work instead. In her shadow, North discovered a more authentic, integrative way to be a spiritual being. Now she works with other empaths, guiding them to explore their own shadows on the path to wholeness.

Foreword writer **Danielle Dulsky** is author of *The Holy Wild* and *Woman Most Wild*.

MORE BOOKS for the SPIRITUAL SEEKER

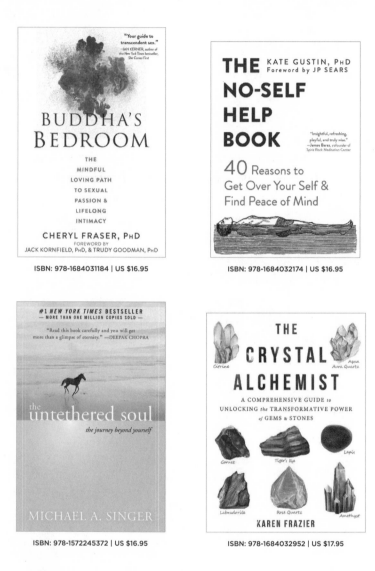

ISBN: 978-1684031184 | US $16.95

ISBN: 978-1684032174 | US $16.95

ISBN: 978-1572245372 | US $16.95

ISBN: 978-1684032952 | US $17.95